Doing What Scientists Do

Second Edition

Doing What Scientists Do

Children Learn to Investigate Their World

Second Edition

Ellen Doris

HEINEMANN
Portsmouth, NH

Heinemann
361 Hanover Street
Portsmouth, NH 03801–3912
www.heinemann.com

Offices and agents throughout the world

The author and publisher wish to thank those who have generously given permission to reprint borrowed material:

Excerpt from *Young Geographers* by Lucy Sprague Mitchell. Copyright © 1971 by Bank Street College of Education. Reprinted by permission of the publisher.

Excerpts from "Keeping Wonder Alive" by Ellen Doris were originally published in *Holistic Education Review,* Volume 5, No. 3, (Fall 1992). Published by Holistic Education Press. Reprinted by permission of the publisher.

Library of Congress Cataloging-in-Publication Data
Doris, Ellen
   Doing what scientists do : children learn to investigate their world /
Ellen Doris.—2nd ed.
       p. cm.
   Includes bibliographical references.
   ISBN-13: 978-0-325-01245-2
   ISBN-10: 0-325-01245-8
   1. Science—Study and teaching (Elementary)—United States. I. Title.
   LB1585.3.D67 2020
   372.3'5044—dc22   2009046728

Editor: Victoria Merecki
Production: Sonja S. Chapman
Typesetter: Newgen Imaging
Cover design: Jenny Jensen Greenleaf
Manufacturing: Steve Bernier

Printed in the United States of America on acid-free paper
19 18 17 16 15 VP 3 4 5 6 7

For Bob

Contents

Acknowledgments

The chance to revisit and revise one's work is a rare one, and I thank Heinemann for the opportunity. In particular, I am indebted to Robin Najar for sustaining this project over the long haul and to Victoria Merecki and Sonja Chapman for managing its completion. I thank those who offered feedback on the original edition or subsequent drafts, especially Barney Balch, Carol Berner, Eleanor Duckworth, Lindy Elkins-Tanton, Eric Johnson, Candace Julyan, Fiona Hughes-McDonnell, Susan Rauchwerk, David Sobel, Bob Strachota, and Jeff Winokur. Many thoughtful educators have fueled my thinking about teaching and learning, drawing, science, and schools in ways that helped this book, among them Peggy Clark, Bud Lichtenstein, Sally Middlebrooks, Trudie Luck Roberts, Carol Rodgers, Ellen Schwartz, Steve Seidel, Joan Strachota, Bonnie Tai, and the members of the Bennington Inquiry Group. I am grateful to all.

I am indebted to the Greenfield Center School for being a place where I could try out ideas and learn from children, parents, and colleagues. Many of the instances described in the following pages took place there. Ruth Charney, Marlynn Clayton, Terry Kayne, Jay Lord, Sue O'Reilly, Chris Pinney, Deb Porter, Brian Sabel, Timmy Sheyda, Jane Stephenson, Bob Strachota, and Chip Wood are among the Center School teachers who encouraged my experiments, worked alongside me in classrooms, made room for my graduate research projects, discussed their own science teaching, or shared photographs and other records of children's explorations. Claudia Hall and Sharon Weiss made particular contributions as interns. Experiences in the Amherst Regional Public Schools, the University of Hartford, and The Common School have also furthered my thinking and writing. I continue to appreciate the many individuals who, along with the Northeast Foundation for Children, brought about the first edition.

My very fond thanks go to the children—some now grown—who have contributed so much to this book. I am thankful for the support of their families as well.

I am deeply grateful to my family and dear friends for their ongoing support. My father's encouragement has sustained me, even in his absence, and Margaret, Sara, Joan, and John—my sisters and brother—remain ever ready to lend a hand or an ear. Stepsons Dan, Joel, and Gabriel have been cheerleaders from distant corners of the planet, while my children, Micky and Kathleen, have endured this project at close range with loving forbearance. Finally and again, my heartfelt thanks to my husband, Bob, my close colleague in this work and my partner in all else.

Introduction

Years ago, on a snowy Saturday morning, I met with fellow teachers in an elementary school classroom. We had assembled for a workshop I was facilitating, and as we shifted from coffee to business, I posed a question: "If, through teaching science, you could give the children in your classroom just one or two important things, what would you give them?" Responses were quick in coming.

"I'd give children the freedom to question!"

"I want them to be more aware of the natural world . . . and for that awareness to enhance, not diminish, their sense of wonder."

"I'd like them to develop a healthy respect and responsibility for nature."

"I'd give them the eagerness to investigate! And patience—to be able to wait and look."

One teacher hoped to impart curiosity. Another cared about communication. A third focused on resourcefulness and the ability to investigate. "When they come upon something new," she explained, "I want them to have lots of different avenues open for learning about it."

Each of us had identified something deeply important. We valued the children we taught and the world around us. We wanted to strengthen the connection between the two. Some of us believed that teaching science could be a way to do so. We had already witnessed the interest our students took in their surroundings and seen how eager they were to share it.

"They're always bringing in their rocks and caterpillars and seashells," a teacher commented. "I want to know how to help them develop that interest." Others lacked this experience. "Frankly, I don't teach science," one confessed. "When I was in school, I always thought science was boring. And I still think it's boring! But I'm ready for someone to convince me it's not."

Of course, I wanted to convince her. I also longed to help the rest of the teachers realize their aims. So, for a number of weekends, I presented them with activities to try and questions to consider. I asked them to explore the physical properties of oil, water, and other kitchen liquids and to study bones and bugs. On intervening school days, we each carried out similar activities with children. These ventures were rewarding, but not universally so. Two teachers tried a particular science activity in their classrooms, and while one maintained that her students showed great interest, the other found that children weren't especially responsive. One teacher was able to get children intrigued with some plants she had grown but had trouble finding information that addressed their questions. Another felt self-conscious when a colleague entered her room during a science lesson. While the children's enthusiasm was unmistakable, the accompanying noise and mess were extreme. Reflecting on these situations, we drew the obvious conclusion: articulating basic goals for science study is one thing; realizing them with actual children is quite another.

Undaunted, we continued to experiment and to discuss the results. The issues we considered that winter—how to structure science activities, respond to children's initial efforts, and encourage further investigation—guided the construction of the original edition of *Doing What Scientists Do*. So did the idea that focusing on actual, ordinary instances of science teaching could be useful in developing practice. I based the book on examples from my own work with children, not because they offered a perfect model but because they were a ready source of specifics to reflect on and react to. As such, they could become a point of departure for others. I hoped *Doing What Scientists Do* would serve teachers who wanted to strengthen the connection between children and the natural world but were unsure how to initiate the process. I also hoped it would serve teachers who had a science program in place and were searching for ways to give children's ideas and questions a more central role.

Among the challenges at the core of the book were:

- How to begin.
- How to get children to pay attention to everyday objects and phenomena.
- How to help children listen to, and learn from, one another.
- How to help children raise and pursue their own questions.
- How to interpret children's statements, written work, and drawings.

These are basic to the present edition as well.

Inquiry Science, the Standards, and Classroom Challenges

Four years after the original publication of *Doing What Scientists Do*, the *National Science Education Standards* were first released. A year later, in 1996, they appeared in final form. The *Standards* drew attention to science education and focused efforts to improve it by presenting a vision for teachers and students to work toward. That vision, like the ones held by teachers who participated in my winter workshop, valued children's sense of wonder and eagerness to investigate. It demanded programs in which students learn science "by actively engaging in inquiries that are interesting and important to them" and teachers who focus children's attention on actual phenomena, facilitate their investigations, nurture their collaborations, and allow them to make significant decisions about the direction their work will take (National Research Council 1996, 13, 31–33, 43–46).

The *Standards* have been a strong voice of encouragement to teachers who believe that children can take an interest in the world around them, explore aspects they are curious about, and learn through doing so. They have also been a major influence on educational policy and curriculum development. Many states now mandate inquiry science programs for elementary school children, and a wealth of wonderful resource books, science kits, and other materials have been developed to support implementation. Even so, few communities boast schools where children's experiences and the questions that spring from them are the mainstay of elementary science. While many teachers long to help children become enthusiastic, competent, and knowledgeable through engaging in real research, they don't always meet with success.

Sometimes, the reason has roots in their relation to the subject matter of science. Many teachers feel too unfamiliar with the material world themselves to serve as guides to it, even when the "tourists" are young children. In an earlier era, these teachers might have managed their discomfort by focusing on the few topics they knew most about. However, the current *Standards* and the state guidelines derived from them specify a wide range of content for children to understand. Ready or not, teachers are asked to tackle this material.

A second reason is linked to teachers' sense of what it means to teach elementary science, a sense often forged by their own experiences as learners. Those who remember choosing their own projects, designing experiments, and doing fieldwork with an enthusiastic teacher are often eager to provide similar opportunities for their students. Those who remember confusing procedures, boring textbooks, or pressure to come up with the right answer have less useful models. Whether they lack pedagogical know-how alone or knowledge of nature as well, concern about their capacity to facilitate children's inquiries leads some to rely heavily on "teacher-proof" curricula. Others simply avoid teaching science.

Even if teachers are comfortable with science, have access to appropriate resources, and are willing to try something new, there may still be difficulties. The need to "cover" twenty chapters in a science text each year has abated in many elementary schools, but even more extreme pressures have taken its place. The current educational climate is a tense one in which high-stakes tests and the potential consequences of low scores cast a shadow for teachers, administrators, and children. Preparing children for literacy and math examinations leaves little time for scientific investigation. Further, while many states now check on children's progress in science through standardized tests, this process can limit the freedom teachers feel to pursue children's interests and questions. Teachers geared toward particular tests may be reluctant to accommodate interests that "won't count" or may not even notice they exist. A teacher who successfully avoids "teaching to the test" may still be consumed by the effort to make sure that every one of her students learns each of the fundamental science concepts specified for her grade level. As my colleague Carol Berner puts it, "If the standards are too loud in your head, you might not hear what the children are wondering about."

Finally, the individual needs of students—and their sheer numbers—must be reckoned with. All too often, when teachers try to implement "inquiry science," the classroom management problems that arise cause them to give up in frustration. Some may continue with their efforts but feel unsure of what children are learning. The open-ended questions and opportunities for independent investigation a teacher provides may prove to be exciting challenges for some children, while others flounder or wander or can't quite make sense of things. The guidance of standards and the availability of appropriate materials are not enough to make a science program work, for the way we introduce materials will determine whether we can find them at the end of the week, and the way we structure activities and respond to individuals will affect children's interest and focus. Teaching science in a classroom of twenty or thirty children requires careful attention to many things. In addition to acquiring a broad understanding of science, teachers must think about specific content and consider the special needs and interests of many children when planning curriculum. We must develop techniques that will foster inquiry, maintain an effective physical environment, and deal with issues of management and discipline. It is a tall order, but not an impossible one. *Doing What Scientists Do* supports those who take it on by describing some basic structures and ways of interacting that can help teachers bring children and the natural world face-to-face and build children's ability to notice, wonder, and pursue questions. Classroom dialogue, along with children's drawings and writing, both exemplify and raise questions about these.

Guiding Beliefs

In this book I present an approach to teaching elementary school science that can help children feel interested in the world around them and able to find out about that world. Here are the beliefs that guide my approach:

Science is a process of inquiry and investigation. It is a way of thinking and acting, not just a body of knowledge to be acquired by memorizing facts and principles.

Familiar, everyday phenomena provide a rich focus for science study. Direct experience with the plants, animals, and objects that surround them enables children to think scientifically and draw conclusions from firsthand observations. Books and other sources can enrich, but not replace, such experience.

Children learn through their own activity. They develop understanding of the world by observing, describing, questioning, and searching for answers.

Teachers can also be active investigators. Teachers can share their own curiosity and interest in the world around them, puzzling about phenomena and exploring along with children.

Applying knowledge of child development contributes to science teaching. Understanding how children at different ages think and act is important in planning, interpreting, and responding to their science work.

A balance between structure and freedom in the classroom is important. By balancing open-ended exploration and focused investigation, teachers create a stable classroom environment that can incorporate activities initiated by children as well as those teachers design or direct.

Each class member has an important contribution to make. Teachers must work to create an inclusive climate in which every child can make discoveries, share information, and offer ideas and insights.

Collaboration is important. Partnerships can be forged between classmates, between teacher and students, and between members of the class and people outside it. Just as scientists thrive on the exchange of ideas, children also benefit from working cooperatively.

About This Edition

This second edition of *Doing What Scientists Do* supports elementary school teachers by describing ways to structure space, activities, and interactions so that children can observe, raise questions, and figure things out. It is not a comprehensive methods manual or curriculum guide, nor does it demonstrate how to address all of the interesting science content suitable for a particular grade level. Rather, it considers some teaching practices that can make inquiry science possible.

Promoting inquiry is a central charge of the *National Science Education Standards*. Many other specific expectations emerge from the *Standards* as well, and when approached as a "To Do" list, these can overwhelm. However, when considered in the context of everyday classroom activity, the *Standards* become a more "user-friendly" guide. With this in mind, I have pointed out links between the *Standards* and various examples in the following chapters. These connections are highlighted and set apart from the main text.

According to the *Standards*, "all science depends on the ultimate sharing and debating of ideas" (NRC 1996, 31–32). Children can draw their ideas as well as say them.

Readers familiar with the first edition of *Doing What Scientists Do* will note that much has been preserved in the current edition. The beliefs that guide my approach are the same, and so are many of the specific instances I use to illustrate this approach. Chapters 1 (Perspective) and 2 (Creating a Context for Science Instruction) contain material originally presented in Chapter 1 (Beginning) and Chapter 2 (Creating an Environment for Science in the Classroom). Chapter 3 (One Way to Begin) includes the initial science meetings and guinea pig observations described in former Chapters 3–5. The description and transcripts have been condensed to make room for a new Chapter 4 (Another Way to Begin). Chapter 4 now presents a way of initiating science that does not call attention to the work of professional scientists but rather focuses children directly on a particular object, organism, or event. Chapter 5 (Building a Culture of Collaboration) discusses ways to teach the skills and practices that encourage respectful communication. It also focuses on how to help children consider a range of ideas, examine assumptions, and deal with problems that arise. Some of this material appeared in Chapters 5 and 6 of the first edition and some of it is new. Throughout, I have tried to distinguish the aspects of particular teaching practices, noting which serve social or institutional goals and which promote scientific thinking.

Chapter 6 (Helping Children Pursue Their Questions) contains some of the information and examples that appeared in the earlier version (Extending Science Work: Teacher as Facilitator). New ideas and examples replace some of the original material, including a list of basic practices that help children frame and investigate questions. Chapter 7 (Drawing as Inquiry) is entirely new, and explains how and why I merge drawing with elementary science. The observation records pictured and described in Chapter 7 of the original edition have been retained, along with a slightly revised discussion of assessment, and can now be found in Chapter 8 (Reviewing Children's Work). Likewise, the essential information about planning and managing field trips from the first edition has been revised and retained. It is now in Chapter 9 (Fieldwork) along with some thoughts about the value of scheduling frequent trips to familiar places. The final chapter of the book has been trimmed to its essential message: teachers, too, can learn through firsthand investigation, and we must seek constructive support for our efforts.

A Note About the Examples

The instances of elementary science in this book emerge from my own experience in schools. I have been a "lone" teacher with a group of twenty-odd students, a co-teacher sharing responsibility for a class with a colleague, and a mentor paired with a student teacher. I have also facilitated elementary science activities as a volunteer, consultant, and graduate student. For ease of reading, I keep discussion of these variations to a minimum in the text and speak as "teacher" throughout. Dialogue has been minimally edited to ensure clarity yet convey what actually took place, and children's names have been changed to protect their privacy.

Most of the examples feature students between the ages of five and ten, although I have worked with children outside of that age range, and with adults, in a similar fashion. The science content is restricted as well. Familiar plants and animals dominate, with guinea pigs and crickets in the spotlight. My lopsided selections were not meant to imply that other subject matter is unimportant or ill-suited to the approach I describe. Rather, they represent the intersection of my wish to consider specifics with the moments I had managed to document. Topics in chemistry, physics, and the earth sciences fascinate children, and, under other circumstances, might well have been the focus of this book.

1 *Perspective*

Teaching science begins with planning.

For me, the first stage of planning is a time for daydreaming, toying with possibilities, and talking with other teachers. It is also a time to consider some fundamental questions. What is science? How do children learn? What can children gain from studying science in school?

Given the practical demands of teaching, this may seem a rather philosophical place to begin. September will bring a room full of children, and a thousand things must be accomplished in preparation for their first day. Classroom furniture must be put in order, and materials and supplies must be located and organized. There are field trips to schedule, files to set up, meetings to attend, and new institutional expectations to adjust to. Every bit of it is essential, but first, I need to establish my sense of purpose and direction. I want specific decisions about what, how, and where children will study to stem from my basic convictions about science, children, and learning.

My convictions—presented here as answers to the questions posed above—form one perspective on teaching elementary science. They are the basis for the approach described in this book. Each teacher will develop an individual perspective based on experience, priorities, attitudes about science, guidance from thoughtfully developed standards, and personal goals for children. This perspective is grounding and makes navigating the daily swirl of details, decisions, and external demands more manageable.

What Is Science?

Science is a way of thinking and acting. It is a process of inquiry and investigation that helps us learn things about ourselves and our surroundings. These things—our scientific facts, principles, and laws of nature—represent knowledge of enormous value. Yet, as Eleanor Duck-

Figure 1–1   Scientists in the classroom

worth reminds us, "the essence of science is not the simple statement of principles, but rather the struggle to find out about the material world" (1978, 1) (Figures 1–1 and 1–2). Science is distinguished by the nature of this struggle as much as it is defined by its subject matter, natural phenomena.

What does the struggle involve? Physicist Morris Shamos (1995, 46) gets to the heart of it, claiming that "science boils down in the end to asking the proper questions of nature and making sense of the answers." He stresses, however, that ordinary ways of asking don't reveal what causes natural phenomena. To find the underlying reasons for what we observe, we need "formal contact with nature." This formal contact—our science—includes observation and description but doesn't stop there. Ultimately, it involves creating theories or models that explain our observations and experience.

In science, explanations are believable only to the extent that they are consistent with actual evidence. How do scientists gather the evidence they require? Through observation and experiment—in other words, by questioning nature in particular ways. The assumption that a statement about nature can be verified objectively, through well-designed, controlled experiments, is what sets science apart from other disciplines. (Shamos 1995, 47; also see NRC 1996, 200–201).

The body of knowledge that results from scientific investigation is an expanding, evolving one. It is a human construction, continually added to and altered as new technologies, insights, and connections cause people

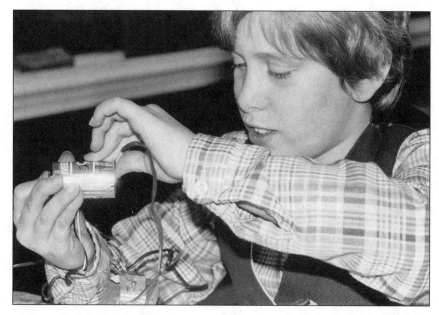

Figure 1–2   "The essence of science . . . is the struggle to find out about the material world." (Duckworth 1978)

to refine and revise their ideas. An oceanographer told me a story about dinoflagellates (a group of microscopic organisms often classified with the algae) that illustrates this point.

Most dinoflagellates live in the ocean, where they propel themselves about with two tail-like flagella. Some are bioluminescent, and when the water surrounding them is disturbed (by the action of waves or by splashing feet), they sparkle and glow. Some dinoflagellates are toxic. When present in large numbers, they form the "red tide" that kills fish and makes shellfish unsafe to eat.

In the early 1900s, paleobotanists (who study fossil plants) furthered our understanding of dinoflagellates by describing and naming the various fossil species they found in marine sediments. These long-dead microorganisms lacked flagella, as soft structures that decay easily are not often preserved in the fossil record, but they were recognizable nonetheless. Decades later, geologists extended the work. As they analyzed sediment cores obtained from the ocean floor, the fossil dinoflagellates these contained contributed new information about the ancient environment.

Meanwhile, marine biologists, who focus on living things in the sea, were also studying dinoflagellates. One thing they did was collect the tiny organisms that caused red tide and culture these in laboratories. Through doing so, biologists learned that some dinoflagellates have rather complicated life cycles involving different phases. Sometimes, they swim around. At other times, they lose the flagella that propel them and "encyst." Without the ability to move, they sink down and settle on to the ocean floor. Laboratory observations revealed that the tiny organisms could shift between these two states, encysting and excysting as environmental conditions changed.

At some point, a geologist examining sediment cores discovered a surprising number of what appeared to be fossil dinoflagellates in the upper layer of sediment. This seemed odd. Fossils, it stood to reason, should be down deep, buried under the many layers of silt that had settled since they died. Suspicious, he brought a few of these "fossils" into the laboratory and tried to culture them. Lo and behold, they excysted, releasing cells that had "tails" and swam about!

It was a surprising and confusing discovery. For years, geologists and biologists had been studying the very same organisms, but they hadn't ever realized it. The "fossil" dinoflagellates and the living, swimming ones had seemed distinct. Each group of scientists had labeled the organisms according to its own naming system, and so many species now had two different names. Differences had to be reconciled, and new paradigms worked out. One insightful observation by a broad-minded scientist had put two sets of scientific "truths" on a collision course.

This story, like many stories of scientific discovery, underscores the fact that scientific knowledge, even when derived from years of meticulous research, is always "tentative and provisional" (Shamos 1995, 51). It counters the image of scientific knowledge as a static collection of truths, an image that unfortunately persists in many elementary classrooms. A first-grade teacher, reflecting on her own early education, lamented, "I thought learning science just meant memorizing all these facts! Scientists were the people who had all the answers!" If scientists had all the answers, of course, there wouldn't be any science left to do. The quest continues, and answers are often elusive.

How Do Children Learn?

Many different theories describe aspects of children's growth and development, including how children learn. These theories can provide valuable insight into the needs and abilities of children at different ages and help us plan and reflect on classroom activities. Understanding their implications for education, testing them against our experience, and deciding which to focus on and put to use can be invigorating. It can also be overwhelming. Developing a thorough familiarity with varied theoretical perspectives and "keeping up" with current research while continuing to meet the demands of a full-time teaching job is a practical impossibility.

Fortunately, teachers can proceed with science instruction anyway, since children have ways of letting us know what they think and what they need. Blank looks, laughter, frustration, and excitement all inform. Sensitivity to such responses allows teachers to work as researchers in the classroom, observing children carefully, listening to what they say, and noting whether our intervention baffles a student or results in a step forward. Theory and research can guide practice, but only our careful attention to the particular children we serve will tell us what they find interesting or puzzling, what they understand, and how they might build on what they know.

In my science work with children, I find it helps to keep a few basic ideas about children and learning in mind. These ideas, distilled from reading and personal experience, help me formulate plans and interpret children's responses.[1] (I sometimes forget a key point. When I do, a child, through her actions, is sure to remind me.)

Children learn by doing. Children construct knowledge as they act upon objects, interact with other people, and try to make sense of their experience. As a science teacher, I must remember that children learn most effectively as a result of their own effort, action, and struggle to understand. Reading and listening have an important place in the science curriculum, but real familiarity with the natural world can't be absorbed from textbooks or lectures. Children need firsthand experience with materials, organisms, and natural phenomena. Opportunities for direct investigation are essential.

Constructing knowledge requires collaboration. Children benefit from considering one another's observations, questions, and points of view. In classrooms where children exchange information and ideas with one another, everyone's thinking gets a push. I try to create opportunities for collaboration and to cultivate the social skills that make it possible. Scientists may spend long hours working alone, but they also rely on others. They read one another's publications, replicate one another's experiments, and relate new ideas to previous theories. They team up to solve problems, conduct research, and discuss findings. This balance of independent and group work can be a model for the classroom.

Children's behavior and thinking develop over time. Children at different ages (or at different stages of development) have characteristic ways of thinking and behaving. Particular issues may be important at

1. Helpful sources include Duckworth 1978 and 1996; Erikson 1950; Piaget 1980; Wadsworth 1978; and Wood 1994.

one age and not at another. Children learn best when teachers take into account the particular characteristics of their age group.

Children are individuals. Individual children have particular strengths, interests, needs, and learning styles. Some children benefit especially from structured situations with clear guidelines, while others thrive in more open-ended learning environments. Even on a narrowly defined task, individual approaches emerge. Children learn best when teachers appreciate "who they are" and teach accordingly.

Teaching a collection of individuals is not simply a matter of catering to different interests and learning styles in a general way. While it is helpful to anticipate a wide range of previous experience and comfort with each new topic we introduce, it is also important to discover, specifically, what each child notices and wonders about as he works. The idiosyncratic way in which each individual makes sense of a shared class experience matters as well.

Children are continually revising their understanding of the world. As children explore their surroundings, test ideas, consider what others tell them, and make new connections, they alter their picture of "the way things work." As adults, we do the same: the process never ends. Any person's knowledge is a work in progress, as is the body of scientific knowledge constructed by professional researchers.

This is easier to accept in theory than in practice, especially if high-stakes testing is a major feature of the educational landscape in which we find ourselves. As teachers, we may worry when children discard faulty notions in favor of more adequate—but still flawed—ideas. We may try to correct a child's conception by telling her what she should think, or feel critical of our efforts if an assessment reveals any lingering confusion. Evaluating our teaching is worthwhile. However, it is important to do so with some acceptance of the fact that children will leave each school year with both naïve perceptions and sophisticated understanding. We must provide the time, materials, suggestions, and interactions that enable children to build up a network of ideas about the world. We can also trust them to add to that network throughout their lives.

Feelings are part of learning. There are emotional, attitudinal, and aesthetic aspects of learning as well as intellectual ones. It is thrilling to peer through a microscope and see a tiny animal that you hadn't known existed or view one of your very own cells! The colors and forms characteristic of different crystals are as beautiful as they are intriguing. Like most teachers, I try to plan science experiences that are fun and fascinating. I also know that frustration, confusion, and other difficult emotions will emerge from time to time: these are potential elements of any real "struggle to find out." It isn't possible to evade all difficulties; it *is* possible to help children accept, weather, and learn from those they encounter.

What Can Children Gain from Studying Science in School?

Science is a dynamic and complex enterprise, and I want to bring it into the classroom as such. I want to see children noticing things, raising questions, investigating: doing what scientists do. But why? Certainly there are external mandates and recommendations that cannot be ignored. However, my real reason for giving science a central place in the curriculum is more personal. As a teacher, my most basic goal is to help children become interested in the world around them and able to find out about that world. I want them to leave my class feeling curious, with the confidence and ability to pursue the puzzles they encounter. Elementary science furthers that aim.

Helping children develop interest, curiosity, or wonder is important. It is also complicated. I've watched many children become focused, lively,

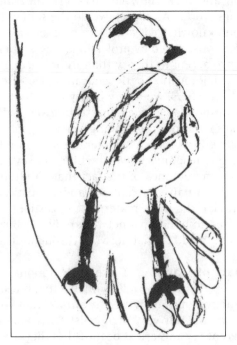

Figure 1–3   "He chased after my hand when I pet it!"

questioning, and thoughtful when presented with organisms or objects to observe (Figure 1–3). But other responses are also familiar, including "Oh, this again," "Yuck!" and "I'm bored." Children have told me they're "done" after giving only brief and superficial attention to a specimen or situation. Others have appeared busy and invested from a distance but on close inspection have proved directionless or vague. Many factors can be responsible. Children may be accustomed to more dazzling, less demanding, entertainment than school science provides. Television programs require little of the viewer. Episodes are timed for short attention spans or rely on explosions, car chases, and other extraordinary drama to keep children involved. Electronic games are more interactive but can be similarly "geared up." In comparison, a soil sample or caterpillar may appear rather dull. Some children may have learned a passive approach to schoolwork; if questions have always been framed by the teacher, students may not know how to come up with their own. They may not even trust that they are free to. Others may simply lack the active strategies required to investigate a problem.

Interest, I believe, requires some confidence in yourself. You have to deem your own observations and questions worthwhile and suspect that you can figure out more if you try. If questions rarely lead to understanding, then some children may conclude that it is better not to be curious.

Back in 1934, educator Lucy Sprague Mitchell described the situation of the children she taught:

> Modern children are born into an appallingly complicated world. A three-year-old in a city environment may be whisked to his steam-heated nursery in an electric elevator, fed from supplies which are ordered by telephone, sent up in a dumb-waiter and stored in an electric refrigerator; he may be taken to a hole in the sidewalk and borne rapidly on an underground train to a distant place. The forces which move his elevator, warm his nursery, extend his mother's voice to a grocery store, cool his milk, propel the subway train, are complicated and difficult to understand, not only at three, at six, at nine, but even at forty. Most of them are hidden from him: indeed, they may be hidden from his parents. He lives in a world of end-products with the functioning causes largely concealed. He is likely to grow up so used to unexplained end-products that he does not form the habit of seeking for causes, for underlying relationships. Which is a round-about way of saying, that so far as this functioning aspect of his environment is concerned, he is likely to grow up without thinking, without opportunity for experimentation. . . . Nowadays a country child as well as his city and suburban brothers is likely to grow up without understanding or even questioning many familiar things—without thinking so far as the

Figure 1–4   **Young children experiment with paint at the easel**

functioning aspect of his world is concerned. And be it said once more, the grown-ups closely associated with these modern children may accept their environment with an attitude almost equally unchallenging. (1971, 12–13)

Today's "modern children" are also born into a complicated world. That does not mean it must remain unexamined and inexplicable. Science, even the kind of science that young children are capable of, offers ways to structure our contact with our surroundings and our thinking about them. This is enough to transform an "appallingly complex world" into one that is intriguing and, in many ways, knowable. Children are not professional scientists, and there is no need to impose the rigorous standards of the profession on them. However, children can benefit from regular contact with natural phenomena and from formalizing that contact somewhat. Teachers can provide students with materials and experiences that provoke their curiosity and questions. We can follow up by helping them devise investigations and ways to consider results that are appropriate to their age and experience.

Perspective in Practice

Many chances to do science arise in a day. So do moments to apply what we understand about science, children, and learning. For example, five- and six-year-olds are quick to propose plans of action:

"Can I mix these paints together?"

"Can we put these beads in the water table?"

"My flower needs more water. Can I fill the jar all the way to the top?"

"Can we get the guinea pig out and read him a story?"

For the most part, answers to such questions can be simple:

"You want to see what happens? Sure, go ahead."

"Your flower needs water? You can take care of that."

There are, of course, other possible responses:

"If you mix all the paints, you'll be all out of blue when you need it."

"These beads are made of wood and they will float. But keep them out of the water table. They'll get damaged."

"Your flower is getting plenty of water already. See, the stem reaches down to the bottom where the water is."

"Our guinea pig can't understand stories. Why not just leave him in the cage?"

Reasonable answers, perhaps, but though they spring readily to mind, I try not to let them leak out.

With this age group, it is important to reward children's initiative. The projects they initiate don't always make sense to me. I don't see why a flower needs water "right up to the top," and I miss the colorful tempera paintings that give way to those brownish-gray, grayish-brown, and mauve creations that are the end result of some paint-mixing experiments. But if I want children to feel able to try out their own ideas and

Figure 1–5 Talking to the guinea pig

develop a sense of purpose, I need to support them with a yes when it is safe and reasonably practical to do so. I work to help children think and act scientifically, but I also try to remember the limits of young children's thinking. Sometimes, children can carefully report actual observations of the guinea pig: he drinks water, he eats, he has no tail. Other times they know he wants to hear a story. The paints can be mixed and the beads dropped in the water table, and children will be quick to note what happens. However, expecting children's predictions to match the results of these experiments is unrealistic: imagining the outcome is no substitute for actually carrying out the proposed action.

Although older children also initiate projects, their thinking is more sophisticated. They are able to plan and reason in new ways, make comparisons, devise simple investigations, and draw more logical conclusions from their observations. One day during cleanup time eight-year-old Carrie was sweeping the floor and bumped into the art table, knocking an old soda bottle full of wildflowers onto the floor. It broke. I went to clean it up, and Carrie moved closer to watch. I gingerly picked up a large piece of glass with "deposit" still visible in raised letters. Before I could place it in the paper bag with the other fragments, Carrie interrupted. "Can I have that?"

"This broken glass? What do you want it for?"

"Well, you know sea glass? Sometimes it has writing like that. I was wondering, maybe we could make sea glass."

I was intrigued by her idea but concerned about the mess. "Let me finish cleaning this up. I don't want anyone to get hurt. If you go get me a box, I'll wrap this piece up so we can store it safely. We can talk more about your idea when all the glass is swept up."

Later on, I inquired, "How do you think sea glass is made?"

"Well," Carrie began, "in the ocean, there's water and salt, and the glass gets worn smooth."

The sight of the glass on the classroom floor had triggered an image and a puzzle. The image—a piece of sea glass, worn and cloudy. The puzzle—how did it get that way? I was eager to continue the conversation.

"So the water and salt get to work on the glass?"

"I think so." Carrie nodded tentatively.

"And what is it you'd like to try with this glass?"

"Well, we could put it, no, a little piece of it, with some water. Maybe it would change."

"Do you need any special kind of water?" I asked.

"Well, we can't get ocean water!" Carrie laughed, acknowledging our inland location. "We could put regular water in, and some salt."

"Those are both things we have at school," I offered. "Then what would you do?"

"Look at it every day. I could see if anything's happened."

I went over her steps. "So you'll put a small piece of this bottle in a container with water and salt and watch to see if it changes to sea glass?" Carrie nodded.

Together we figured out a safe way to break off a small piece of the glass for her experiment, and she got to work setting it up. I imagined the results might lead her to consider new factors, such as how time and motion help form beach treasures.

Again, things could have proceeded differently. When the bottle broke, all I saw was a dangerous mess. I wanted it cleaned up and safe. When Carrie said, "Can I have that?" my first thought was, "Of course not! You could get hurt!" But I felt I should at least find out what was on her mind. When she proposed making sea glass, I was intrigued, but did not simply respond, "You want to make sea glass? Sure, give it a try!" My experience with eight-year-olds has taught me that they are full of ideas and quick to suggest projects. Often, the ideas range from big to grandiose.

"We want to write a book. It's going to be about all of the different birds of prey in the world."

"I think our class should build a model of the pond we've been visiting. A scale model. We'll make it just like the real one, with all the ducks and geese, and the windmill and trees and. . ."

"Our group is writing a play. We're going to put it on in town."

"I want to figure out how things fly."

It is important for eight-year-olds, as well as younger children, to pursue projects they initiate. Experimenting, collecting, constructing,

---

Developing a perspective on science and on how children learn grounds science teaching. Preparing to teach also includes selecting specific content and activities for children to focus on during the course of the year. The *National Standards for Science Education* can guide this selection and also help teachers recognize when children's spur-of-the-moment ideas and questions might be steps toward developing important fundamental concepts. According to the *Standards*, all children should learn about the properties of objects and materials; those in grades K–4 should come to understand that objects have observable properties and the ability to react with other substances (NRC 1996, 127). Carrie's sea glass project was a small step in this direction. It also furthered her ability to ask questions about objects, plan a simple investigation, and propose an explanation—abilities that support inquiry (NRC 1996, 122).

and reading all hold rewards. However, if I simply encourage every big idea that is proposed, some children may fail to anticipate the steps necessary to achieve satisfactory results. If unable to follow through, feelings of failure or frustration may result, rather than a sense of competence. With help, children can draw on their ability to think about real situations, clarify questions, anticipate some problems, and formulate plans. A helpful response to an eight-year-old's proposal is often: "Tell me more about your idea. How do you think you could get to work on that? What will you need? Who can help?"

2 *Creating a Context for Science Instruction*

The context for school science instruction has many dimensions. Some, like the broad economic and political forces that shape educational policy, are beyond teachers' control. Others are well within our domain. We create a classroom context for science by arranging space, materials, and schedule to support interest and inquiry. Furniture, pencils, and paper, while not at the heart of the scientific enterprise, still have an important role to play.

Making a Place

If schools were designed with elementary science instruction in mind, what would classrooms look like? They would be big, for one thing, so that children could set up a stream table, spread out a rock collection, move around and try things out. Each would have plenty of long, flat tables at which to work and a comfortable meeting area where the whole class could sit in a circle. There would be all kinds of tools, equipment, and materials to use and accessible cupboards in which to store them. I'd want a sink, maybe two, a telephone with an outside line, easy access to the outdoors and library, and computers that always worked.

I've never had such a classroom. Few teachers have. So, while it is fun to fantasize, it is also important to make a place for science in the cramped, partially equipped rooms in which we're apt to find ourselves. I like to begin by establishing a small science area. While science can, and will, happen anywhere—on the playground, at the window, or at a child's desk—designating a special place within the room is still helpful. For one thing, it is a visible statement of priorities. Anyone who enters and looks around can see that science is a focus. More important, if a space is always available and "open for business," children can pursue science activities whenever they have time. When children are taught how to work in a designated area with purpose and independence, they

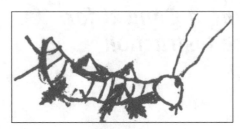

Figure 2–1   **A cricket**

will initiate science study in ways that are meaningful for them—ways we may or may not have considered.

I know this from firsthand experience. One fall my class of seven- and eight-year-olds was studying crickets. We kept the crickets in glass aquariums on the science table, fed them dry dog food, and watered them with tiny sponge-plugged bottles. Miles and Cory came to school each morning, stored their coats and lunches, and headed straight for the science table. They held a regular morning vigil and would take time for another quick look on their way to reading group or recess. During our quiet work period in the afternoon, they often chose to go to the science table and look some more.

During that fall there were many teacher-structured lessons when the science area temporarily expanded to fill the whole room. At those times every child was observing, talking, drawing, and writing about our crickets. The self-chosen, independent work of the two boys differed in some regards. No records were kept; no particular hypotheses were articulated; there were no schedules, no deadlines, no book research. Miles and Cory made time to watch, listen, and pursue their keen interest in their own way. They approached this work with affection and dedication.

Were they leaning anything? I'm convinced they were. At times I'd be working nearby, watching a group paint with watercolors or helping someone with a reading assignment. Miles would motion for me to come and take a look: "See how this one is moving her head? We think that's how she eats."

During whole-class discussions, children often tried to account for the behavior they had witnessed.

"I saw one cricket put its antenna in its mouth!" an amazed eight-year-old reported.

"Lots of them do that," corroborated Cory.

"Maybe they're eating their antennae!" suggested another classmate.

"I don't think so," Cory replied thoughtfully, "because later, it seems like they still have their whole antennae. The antennae don't keep getting shorter." Cory wasn't simply offering an opinion. He had evidence to support his claim. Apparently, he had already encountered this phenomenon and given it some thought.

I was struck by how often the two boys made similar contributions to our discussions, remembering an observation or providing useful data as we considered a hypothesis. Equally important, they were learning to work with independence and purpose, making choices about the direction their learning would take. It would have been more difficult for them to achieve this without ready access to the crickets.

A permanent science area encourages children's involvement in long-term projects and allows teachers to suggest lines of inquiry that don't have a predictable end. If children must put objects or experiments away and out of sight at the end of each work period, ongoing involvement requires anticipation, careful scheduling, and unpacking. Children are not always able to manage these feats to the degree required to follow through on their ideas. As a result, the questions they raise may be forgotten or remain unanswered.

Space to display work is also important. It helps children become aware of and learn from one another's efforts. Alex, age five, taught me this when he proudly brought me his second drawing of our pet guinea pig. The previous week he had not been too pleased with his work (see Figure 2–2a). As we looked together at its long arms and lionlike mane, he had explained with a shrug, "I don't know how to draw guinea pigs yet."

Looking at his second attempt (Figure 2–2b) I commented, "Alex! You really showed the shape of his body in this drawing."

Figure 2–2a   Alex's guinea pig: first attempt

Figure 2–2b   Alex's guinea pig: second attempt

"I used to make them look like people," he explained, "'cause I didn't know how to draw the bodies of animals yet."

"I notice how much your work has changed," I said "How did you learn?"

He pointed to another child's work on the bulletin board. "I looked at Joel's. He didn't say about how to do it, but when I looked, I could tell."

Children can tell other things by looking at displays as well: that a classmate has a plausible explanation for why a pendulum swings in a certain way, or that an unfamiliar creature was just discovered in a drop of pond water.

In planning a permanent science area, I keep in mind the kind of work I want children to be doing and the characteristics and needs of my class. I also factor in how much space is available, the location of other work areas, and the furniture and supplies I have at my disposal.

Figure 2–3 **This science area in a K–1 classroom has space to display specimens and children's work**

Figure 2–4 **A deep windowsill provides handy storage for reference books**

For any age level, I know I want enough room for children to work together. Minimally, this could mean two desks set side by side, with display space on top and clipboards handy for writing. Long tables are great—they allow enough space both to set up displays and to accommodate three to six children (see Figure 2–3). If possible, I put the table in a part of the room where it will be easily noticed—along the middle of a wall or in a place that can be seen from the doorway. I want children to spot a new display right away or to be able to "check in" on the pollywogs as they head off to math group or art. The science area needs to be located where children can concentrate, but not where extreme quiet is always required. In a classroom where various activities take place simultaneously, keep it at some distance from drama, carpentry, or reading tables. It coexists well with art. Reference books need to be located where children can get them quickly, without disrupting other groups (see Figure 2–4). If books are handy, they'll be put to use. If they're far away or hard to find, they won't be.

Windows can be wonderful if you're growing plants, deadly if you're keeping a tank of guppies. Animals need protection from direct sunlight, so find a way to block the windows if need be.

Accessible storage space for supplies such as crayons, hand lenses, clipboards, and paper is important. Children are more able to work with independence when they can find what they need. Finished work also needs a place; baskets, folders, canvas pockets, and drawers all work well. (For additional information on room arrangement, see Clayton 2001.)

In summary, the essential materials and equipment you will need are easy to come by:

- A small table or some desks
- Chairs
- A few transparent containers for housing visiting animals
- Crayons, pencils, and colored pencils
- Blank paper, notebooks, or worksheets

Helpful, but not always necessary, are:

- Hand lenses
- Pocket magnifiers or microscopes
- Clipboards
- Rulers and other measuring tools
- Construction paper

Some Thoughts About Equipment and Materials

Magnifiers and microscopes. Hand lenses can extend children's powers of observation both indoors and out. Most magnify three to six times. Purchase enough hand lenses for each child to have one, or store a small number at the science table for everyone's use. Plastic lenses are most affordable, but glass is less easily scratched.

I love microscopes and the glimpse of worlds-within-worlds they allow. Children seven or eight years old can be introduced to low-magnification microscopes (also called dissecting microscopes or stereo microscopes) (see Figure 2–5). These instruments reveal the surfaces of familiar objects in astonishing detail and enable children to recognize features of plants and animals that would otherwise go unseen. A 30× pocket magnifier with a battery-powered bulb is an affordable, and portable, alternative. Older children can profitably use compound microscopes, which can magnify a specimen 100 or more times. This allows a peek at things as tiny as cells and the structures within them.

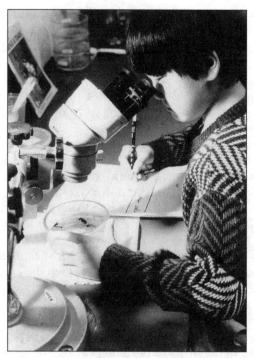

Figure 2–5 Seven or eight years old is a good age for introducing the stereomicroscope

The technical difficulties involved in making slides, together with the degree to which a magnified specimen differs from the naked-eye view, make compound scopes frustrating for most young children. Even older elementary students may need plenty of adult help to master these tools. Microscopes with built-in digital cameras enable a teacher or child to project a specimen so that the entire class can see it at once, enabling collaborative inspection and discussion.

Measuring tools. Some children want rulers to use for drawing straight lines or measuring specimens. Spring scales, pan balances, and other measuring devices will also come in handy. These can be stored in another place and taken out when needed.

 I make rulers and other measuring tools available, but in the early grades I seldom require their use. Children can compare sizes in many ways, noting, "This bone is longer than that one," or "This rock is as big as my hand!" Encourage children to compare and measure, but keep in mind that if they are not yet conserving number, area, or volume, they may size things up quite differently than you do. Likewise, until children can deal easily with the fractional amounts on a ruler or keep track of both ends at once, their measuring motions may yield inaccurate results. As children gain understanding and experience, expectations can be adjusted. If an accurate measurement is important to a group of children who are not yet skilled at making one (as it might be to a group using a field guide that notes size as an identifying attribute), be sure you help them.

Simple display aids. Colored construction paper or poster board is valuable when making displays (see Figure 2–6). It organizes space for children and calls attention to specimens or written directions. Colors can be chosen to present objects attractively and to make them more visible. (Dark paper best displays a white shell, but a light color reveals the thin strands of algae in a glass dish of pond water). Flat boxes with transparent lids, such as Riker Mounts, both exhibit and protect. When the space in a science area is well defined (pencils in the can, specimens arranged attractively on the colored paper), children can keep the area neat and take good care of delicate objects.

Maintaining the science area—keeping it organized and enticing—is worth the effort it takes. In setting up this area, we've said, "Science is important here." If we allow it to collect dust and become cluttered, or if specimens are frequently lost or damaged, we change our message to, "Well—not *that* important!"

Paper, notebooks, and worksheets. Scientists of all ages can keep records. I often make use of blank notebooks or drawing paper for record keeping, and I use worksheets as well. I'll admit to some ambivalence about the term *worksheet*. Its fill-in-the-blank connotations bring reams of dreadful handouts to mind. Worksheets need not stifle children's thinking, however. Good worksheets (or notebook templates) add to the definition of an activity (see Figure 2–7). They indicate ways of approaching and organizing it. This can help children get started, especially if they are accustomed to lots of teacher-directed work requiring them to answer specific questions. Simply sending them off to observe can be too open-ended or vague for some children.

A well-designed worksheet or template will suggest ways to begin and proceed without narrowing children's responses to that "one right answer." It can instead imply, "Note the date and what you looked at," then "Draw what you see," or "Make a prediction." I typically store a few kinds at the science table for children to use if they wish. (Reproducible samples are included in the Appendix.) Eventually, some children will be able to design their own.

When I organize a project for children, I search for a balance between specific direction and open-ended possibility. I want to structure

Figure 2–6a   Colored construction paper helps present objects attractively and defines space so that students can take care of delicate specimens

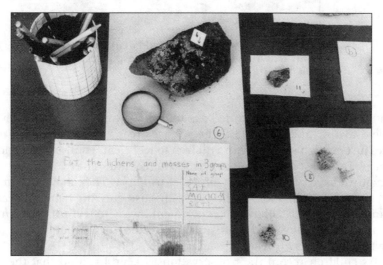

Figure 2–6b   Display of samples students collected on a field trip

the work so that children know what is expected and are able to get engaged. I also want to provide enough freedom for children to work in their own ways and trust their own ideas, priorities, and ways of proceeding. Any record-keeping form can be designed with this balance in mind. On the ones I typically prefer, children can begin by drawing or

Figure 2–7   Good worksheets add definition
to an activity without narrowing responses to
that "one right answer"

writing. They can write a little or a lot, draw a top view, a side view, a
scale drawing, and so on. Like the science area, a good worksheet provides just enough structure for children to feel clear, comfortable, and in
control. It also leaves room to explore. When children have outgrown the
format we have provided, they often let us know. They may come to us
and say, "Can I add another sheet?" "Can I use drawing paper instead?"
"Can I do a report?" "I have an experiment I want to try." At other times
we may realize they need more guidance. Then, forms that break a task
down into a series of clear steps are in order.

As children record their observations, I keep in mind that the finished "product" they create is just one aspect of their work. Product and
process are always intertwined. Drawing or describing an object helps us
see it, as well as conveys what we see to others. Completed records can
help children remember information and provide points of closure. But
ever-continuing inquiry and dialogue are what generate understanding
and excitement.

Children need not record information each time they go to the science area or participate in a science lesson. They can productively spend hours watching pond animals or holding the guinea pig without putting pencil to paper. Drawing and writing are demanding activities, and children also need time to look and to wonder. Requiring a product can help children attend and share, but it can also get in the way. Again, I search for balance, so that "observe" and "investigate" do not come to mean "Fill out a form." (See Campbell and Fulton 2003 and Harlen 2001, for discussions of record keeping and science notebooks.)

Science Kits

Designing a unit of science study and collecting the materials and equipment necessary to carry it out can take tremendous time and thought. Science kits trim preparation significantly. A well-designed kit can also make the prospect of teaching unfamiliar content less daunting by providing background information about the topic, a well-structured sequence of activities for students to follow, and information to help teachers anticipate what students are likely to do and wonder about. Remember, though, that even the best of kits cannot fully equip a teacher or anticipate the particular children with whom it will be used. Teachers must help children build bridges between the kit and the wider world so they can apply new understandings in situations that are not prepackaged.

Over the years I've successfully used kits purchased from supply companies as well as kits assembled by colleagues. The ones I've liked most have the following things in common.

An orienting overview. When I open a science kit, I like a brief introduction that helps me recognize the rest of the things I'll unpack. What is the focus of the kit? Is it an introduction to a particular topic or an advanced unit for children with extensive previous experience? What grade level is it designed for? What aims, broad questions, or standards does it address? Do particular notions about teaching and learning drive its approach? What materials are included and what will children do with them? I like to get the "rhyme or reason" in a nutshell at the start.

Background information about the topic. As I've moved from school to school and grade to grade, I have often been expected to teach a "new" topic. Sometimes it was one I hadn't thought much about before. In such situations it is a comfort to find clearly written information about interesting aspects of the topic. What are some conclusions scientists have reached? What convinced them of these things? Are there particular ways of thinking about or investigating the topic that might make sense to children? Special terms or techniques it is helpful to know? Intriguing facts that can enrich or extend the discoveries students will make for themselves? While getting acquainted with the literature in a kit, keep in mind that printed information about protozoans or light waves is no substitute for encounters with the real thing. I like to try out the activities children will do, then compare what I've read with my own experience.

Information about what children tend to notice and do. If a science kit was field-tested, then its developers learned how different classes responded to its activities and suggestions. Did particular questions usually arise? Did some activities pose special challenges? Did children or teachers think of interesting extensions to try? When you are venturing into new territory, the experience of others can be invaluable. It helps if some of that is included in the kit.

Interesting activities that bring children and phenomena "face-to-face." I want a kit to suggest activities that promote firsthand familiarity with particular phenomena. Activities of this sort encourage children to raise questions of their own. It is important to be alert for these questions and to help children pursue some of them, even if they are not addressed by the kit. It is also important to bear in mind that the activities in a kit may not lead children to broad generalizations. (For example, a child may set up a plastic cup terrarium and learn a great deal about the pill bugs inside, but generalizing about the basic needs of all living things does not necessarily follow.)

A realistic timetable. It is helpful to know that a particular experiment can typically be carried out in half an hour, or that ten forty-minute periods are usually sufficient to move through the kit's basic lessons. It will be possible, and perhaps necessary, to depart from this timetable. Still, it is useful—especially when trying something new—to have a rough schedule mapped out in advance. Many kits offer one.

Other Aspects of Context

The context for school science instruction must offer both freedom to explore and sufficient structure to generate learning. As I work to create such a context, I attend to space and materials. I also keep the following in mind.

Children can become scientists in the classroom. They will learn best if they can observe and study natural phenomena directly. This does not mean that children need a laboratory filled with expensive equipment in order to work, or that eight-year-olds will be able to reason about hypothetical situations that have no connection to their concrete experiences. It does mean that children need to be involved in firsthand exploration of the world around them.

Children need to be able to work together. Partner, small-group, and whole-class activities contribute to both the pleasure and productivity of the class. Room arrangement and furniture can make a range of collaborations possible.

Children will draw from a given experience in ways different from adults and from one another. This happens because of developmental differences, individual knowledge and ways of understanding things, and unique personalities. I try to create experiences that offer a range of possible directions and outcomes and to accept various ways of working and thinking.

Excitement, wonder, questions, and surprises are a part of science. I need to be attentive to what sparks children's interest, what frustrates them, and what they find rewarding. This doesn't mean I exclude everything that is not immediately captivating, easy, and fun from the science curriculum, or that I ignore all external mandates. It does mean that the final curriculum is a negotiated one that reflects particular learners.

Children need plenty of time to work! Observing, making records, designing investigations, and developing and testing ideas all take time. There isn't a way to compress a significant science study into a few brief lessons without eliminating the science in the process. For this reason, it is generally better to pursue a few topics each year than to "cover" tons of material. One year, I spent from September through December studying crickets with a class of seven- and eight-year-olds. Another year, we focused on birds from September through June. Five- and six-year-olds began observing a guinea pig one fall, and he remained the center of their science work for almost two months. In-depth work like this is not possible in many schools, and exposing children to a variety of interesting topics is, of course, important. However, if I find I'm always rushing to get through the list of activities I've selected or been assigned, I start looking for ways to trim the list or adjust the schedule so that children can engage in real inquiry.

Careful organization of the physical environment, selection of materials, and attention to schedule allow children to engage in science. Once the room is ready, my thoughts turn to how I will invite a new group of children to participate.

Creating an environment conducive to inquiry is essential. According to the *Standards*, teachers must "design and manage learning environments that provide students with the time, space, and resources needed for learning science" (see Teaching Standard D, NRC 1996, 43).

---

3 *One Way to Begin*

When school starts in September, I know it will be weeks before my classroom is in full swing. I open special areas of the room one by one and introduce equipment and materials carefully and deliberately. Academic work gears up over time as children become comfortable in this new setting and I become familiar with each child's strengths and needs. While I know this measured pace pays off, I also know that children crave interesting things to think about and do right from the first day. So I begin science promptly, in part because of my own enthusiasm for the content but also because I love the way a shared investigation can captivate a collection of individual children and turn them into a team.

I am of two minds about how to initiate science work. One option is to introduce children to science as a discipline, a way of knowing distinct from other human enterprises such as history, art, or writing literature. When I begin in this way, I frame the specific activity or investigation we undertake in terms of scientific practices and make explicit links between children's schoolwork and the activity of professional scientists. Another option is to put aside all discussion of science and simply study some interesting organism or phenomenon. This "object" gets our whole attention, and children's ways of investigating it are not bound by scientific norms. I discuss the first option in this chapter, the second in Chapter 4.

Each course of action is suited to particular situations. Your own way of thinking about curriculum, your school culture, and the previous experience of your students will shape the way you begin, and you can select and adapt these ideas to fit your own circumstances.

Introducing Five-Year-Olds to What Scientists Do

One fall I met with a group of five-year-olds while the rest of their K–1 class worked independently in other areas of the room. My fledgling scientists sat in a circle in our meeting area, not far from the science table. A large easel holding a flipchart stood where all the children could see it. (I habitually list children's ideas on a chart to promote literacy and record thoughts or decisions we can refer to later.) My aim in this first meeting was to gather children's ideas about scientific work and draw on these ideas to introduce a simple observation activity. I also wanted to make sure children were familiar with the materials set out at our small science table so that they would be able to work there independently.

Ellen D.: Today we're going to start some work that we'll be doing all year long. We're going to start our science work! What are the people who do science work called? They have a special name—what's that name?

Danny: Scientists.

Ellen D.: Scientists. Have you heard that word? (*I write* Scientists *on the chart*.) That's how the word looks. Scientists. Fancy word! Right now, you're going to turn into scientists. What is it that scientists do?

Laurie: They look at things.

Ellen D. (*repeating Laurie's idea as I write, though not intending to parrot.*): They look at things. Yes. What else do they do?

Rachel: They look at bugs.

Ellen D. (*writing*): They look at bugs . . .

Rachel: And they see what kind they are.

Ellen D. (*noticing a raised hand*): Neil, you have an idea.

Neil: They discover things.

Ellen D. They discover things. (*I nod to Alex, who also has his hand up.*)

Alex: They do paintings.

Ellen D. (*unsure what Alex has in mind*): They do paintings. What do you think a scientist might do a painting of?

Alex: Well, maybe sometimes they do weird paintings, like they go down and they go up, then that way, that way, then all around. (*He demonstrates.*)

Ellen D. (*realizing Alex is most likely talking about abstract art but uncertain whether to distinguish it from science at this point*): What would a scientist want to show people in a painting? Or—what might a scientist make a painting of?

Rachel (*conforming Alex's contribution to my topic*): They could make a painting of a bug.

Ellen D.: A scientist might make a painting of a bug to show other people what the bug looked like. (*Though perhaps the case, this is not what Alex meant, and I am unsatisfied with my response.*) Any other ideas?

MICHAEL: Um, a horse.

ELLEN D.: A scientist might make a painting of a horse, if he or she were studying horses. Are there any other kinds of jobs they do? (*I point to our list, hoping not to get bogged down naming all the animals one could paint.*) They might look at things, they might discover things, paint what they see. Do they do any other kinds of work?

NEIL: Um, they might dig up dinosaur bones.

ELLEN D.: They might! Have you ever heard of a scientist digging up dinosaur bones?

NEIL: Yes, I seen a movie of it.

ELLEN D. (*noticing that Neil seems to have more to say*): And you thought of something else.

NEIL: They might fit them together.

ELLEN D.: They might fit them together.

BRIAN: And I saw a real skeleton.

ELLEN D.: They might fit all the bones together and have a skeleton!

I collect a few more ideas and then review the final list. I underline *Scientists look at things* and tell the children we will start our science work in just that way. I write the word *observe* on the chart and ask the children if they have ever heard it before. Many have not, but Neil knows that it means looking at things, and Rachel suggests that the looking must be done carefully. Timmy tells me to draw a box around the word to set it apart from others on the chart. *Observe* becomes part of our shared vocabulary.

Moving on to Observing

Announcing that I will bring the children something to observe, I retrieve a large cage from the science table. "The guinea pig!" several children exclaim. "The second time I've seen it!" offers Michael, well on his way to being an old hand. "I knew it," Danny whispers to his neighbor.

After clarifying that I want the children to study the guinea pig by observing him (but not, as Timmy has suggested, by marking him), I ask what they have noticed. Rachel has seen teeth. "He drinks and he eats," is Timmy's contribution. Wanting the children to distinguish what is happening right now from knowledge gained through books and previous observations, I ask Timmy, "Is that what he's doing right now?" "No," says Timmy, the guinea pig is now "walking around."

I ask other children to share, and I hear, "He's furry," "He nibbles at the cage," "I can see through his ears, and it's dark in his ears."

Laurie comments on the small size of those ears, and I note that a scientist would pay attention to that. But when I ask why that is so, there is no response. The children don't know what I'm driving at—my question demands an ability to generalize that is beyond their age and experience. I try to be more specific and concrete. "Are all animals just the same, with the same kind of ears?"

The children find this idea laughable. "No!" they chorus. The small ears, together with other features they have noticed, are part of what distinguishes this guinea pig from other species. At some level they understand this. Their combined observations describe him well. At that moment, the guinea pig squeaks.

LAURIE (*giggling*): Funny!

ELLEN D.: What did you notice right now?

TIMMY: He took a squeak.

ELLEN D.: Did you notice that from looking at him?

CHILDREN: No.

ELLEN D.: How?

LAURIE: From hearing him.

ELLEN D. (*calling attention to this additional way of collecting information*): So sometimes when scientists observe, they listen. (*Rachel looks like she wants to say something.*) Do you have another thing, Rachel?

RACHEL: There's a log in his cage.

Indeed there is. It's something for the guinea pig to chew on. Michael notes that the guinea pig has whiskers, and Kathleen observes that he scratches. At this point, with our exploration launched, I decide to introduce a simple worksheet that children can use to record their observations.

ELLEN D.: You've been looking and listening and noticing and telling me lots of things you've noticed. But you know what? There's a special way for you to keep track of all the things you notice about our guinea pig. Laurie, I want you to stand up and walk over to the science table. Show everyone where we keep the observation sheets we use for keeping track. (*Laurie crosses to the science table and locates a canvas pocket on the bulletin board.*) Great. Now count out one for each person. (*While she is counting, I turn to the group.*) How many do you think she'll need? Nine, that's a lot!

LAURIE (*returning with a stack*): I don't know if it's the right number.

ELLEN D. (*nodding reassuringly*): Now, Laurie brought you these. This is a special paper that you're going to work on when you do your science observation. Look what it has on it. Up at the top it says, *Name of Scientist*. If this were Rachel's paper, what would go here? (See Appendix for sample record forms.)

I continue to review the form, pointing out a place to draw how the guinea pig looks. "Down at the bottom," I continue, "if you're the kind of scientist who'd like to do some writing, it says *I noticed,* and there's room for you to write. What's something you could write that you noticed?" I do not want to pressure children to write; many are new to school and to writing. Nor is writing the main point of this activity; looking and noticing are. However, I don't want children to avoid recording their observations simply because the worksheet is unfamiliar or difficult to read.

"His ears are little," Timmy volunteers.

I point out the pencils and crayons on the science table nearby, as well as another canvas pocket for finished papers. I want children to be able to manage their own materials so that I am free to discuss their ideas and observations. I send pairs of children off to gather clipboards, crayons, and pencils, then watch as they get settled.

Brian begins quickly—looking at the guinea pig, drawing, looking again. Laurie has a selection of crayons spread out in front of her. She writes her name—each letter a different, beautiful color. Neil holds a clipboard, paper, and pencil as he watches two children in the block area. He continues to stand, but then shifts his gaze to the guinea pig and the other children at work. Alex looks up at me and gestures toward his paper. "Does it go this way?" he asks. I nod. He seeks further assurance, "Is here where I put my name?" I nod again. I notice Timmy, sitting cross-legged, very close to one corner of the guinea pig cage. Tap-tap-tap goes his pencil on the edge of his clipboard. His proximity to the cage and that tapping pencil make me watchful. Brian and Rachel draw with focus. Then Timmy, after a mere five minutes at work, tosses his paper my way.

"I'm done," he announces.

"Come tell me about this work!" I respond. "I see brown here—the color of his fur. And you noticed some things here." I point to the head end of his drawing.

"His eyes and ears and nose," Timmy explains.

I want to refocus Timmy on the guinea pig, yet I don't want to convey that his effort is inadequate. "You noticed all those parts!" I remark. "I'm going to take a look at those eyes." I move closer to the cage. "Did you get a look at the color of his eyes?" Timmy also takes a peek. "Looks black," he says.

"Black eyes. Not like yours!" Timmy's eyes are blue. "How would you show the color of his eyes in your drawing?" He holds up a black crayon, and I nod. "That would really show people what you noticed."

I expect that Timmy will color in the circles he has made for eyes and be "done" again. Perhaps I'll have him stay and watch the guinea pig some more, or I may have him join another group of children somewhere else in the room. Pushing him to attend beyond his capacity is not apt to deepen his interest.

I move around the group, commenting on what children have drawn or said. Occasionally, I attempt to redirect a child who seems to have strayed. Other times, I try to help children extend their observations in small ways.

ELLEN D.: Rachel! I can tell from your drawing you've been noticing the toes of this guinea pig. Could you tell how many he has?

RACHEL: No.

ELLEN D.: Do you want me to pick him up so you can see? (*Rachel nods, and I position the guinea pig so that his feet are easy to see. A number of children stop to watch.*)

RACHEL (*counting the toes on his back feet first*): One, two, three.

ELLEN D.: Three on the back. How about the front?

RACHEL: One, two, three, four. (*Some children look surprised.*)

ELLEN D.: There are four toes on the front but three on the back.

I place the guinea pig back in the cage. Rachel starts to erase some toes on her drawing, revising to include the new data. Meanwhile, Timmy's tapping pencil approaches the cage. Perhaps he will be tempted to poke. I decide to intervene, just in case.

ELLEN D.: Timmy, if your finger or your pencil goes in his cage, what could happen?

TIMMY: He could bite.

ELLEN D.: Ouch! And it could also be scary for him. So fingers and pencils stay where?

TIMMY: Out.

ELLEN D.: Yes. You remember!

After about ten minutes, some children bring me their finished papers (see Figure 3–1). I exchange a few words with each, mentioning something I notice about each drawing or how a child has worked and

Figure 3–1 The children record their observations of the class' guinea pig

giving each a chance to share an observation. Then I offer a choice: "You can stay here and look at the guinea pig some more, and when everyone's through, we can take turns holding him, or you can choose another area in the room to work in." I want kids to enjoy learning about this animal and to consider him in different ways (see Figure 3–2). While I know some children have already stayed with this activity as long as they can, I don't want to give the message that once they have recorded some information there is no point in looking further.

Figure 3–2   Holding the guinea pig

What's Taken Place

The brief meeting described earlier "sets the stage" for the activity that immediately follows and also for future work. Children's ideas about what scientists do include looking at bugs and making weird paintings—a range one can expect in a K–1 class. Generally speaking, five-year-olds will offer fairly literal and specific ideas. They may confuse science with other professions, get sidetracked listing many examples of a particular activity, or tell personal stories. We can gauge how much of this is productive. For five-year-olds, this first science meeting needs to be kept quite short. Ten minutes is enough time to talk about what scientists do, define what the children will do, and consider how to manage materials. It is also about as long as many five-year-olds can stay focused on such matters! However, maintaining this pace for the sake of the group often comes at the expense of particular individuals: some children may not get a turn. I try to be sensitive to this and make time to hear additional ideas as children shift to the next phase of their work. I also may return to a topic in a later meeting, giving new children an opportunity to share.

The observation activity that followed our meeting introduced a simple form of inquiry in which children pay attention to something and notice what it is like. They gather information while looking, drawing, talking. Questions occur, and some of these can be answered by counting, listening, or taking another look. Though I provided little information about the guinea pig, by the end of the short session, the children had discovered much about him—he could squeak, stand, and wiggle his nose, and he has long front teeth, ears of different colors, and more toes on his front feet than on his back. More involved investigations sometimes evolve from these observation sessions. However, they are worthwhile even as stand-alone activities.

Asking questions about objects, organisms, and events in the environment is fundamental to scientific inquiry (NRC 1996, 122). Observing their pet guinea pig puts five-year-olds in a position to do so.

Prompting Older Children to Talk About Science

Children bring something different to their work each year—new understandings, abilities, and experiences. Ideas about what scientists do become more complex and often reflect more knowledge of inquiry and investigation. One six-year-old offered this perspective:

"Well, scientists don't really know everything, which most people think they do, but they don't. What they do is they try to figure out a lot of things, because people think that scientists know everything but they don't. They're trying to know a lot, so they get other scientists to help them, and also usually people figure things out by making mistakes."

"They study insects by spying on them in the woods," a classmate followed. "Well, they don't really spy. They just go in the woods and look around and see what they can figure out about the insects by looking at them. And then they bring them back into their laboratory and study them." When asked what a laboratory was, he responded, "Oh, it's a place where the scientists do all their creations and they study with their microscopes."

Another child added to the image. "Sometimes scientists might have labs bigger than the school because they have tons of things in there and they stay up all night to figure out stuff."

Figuring, studying, creating, making mistakes, and trying to know—these children portray science as a process. That science is something one *does* is also understood by the nine-, ten-, and eleven-year-old girls in the meeting summarized below. Informed by books, television, previous schoolwork, and other experiences, they are familiar with many branches of science as well as with specific problems and research efforts. Despite their sophistication, I am able to use the same basic format I used with the five-year-olds.

ELLEN D.: Today, we're going to start our science work. What is it that scientists do?

BETH: Well, they do research on stuff. And there's different kinds of scientists.

ELLEN D. (*nodding*): There are.

BETH: Lots of different kinds!

ELLEN D.: What are some?

BETH: I don't know—like—entomologists.

I don't require children to use scientific terms, but when they do, I want to make sure that everyone understands what they mean.

ELLEN D.: Entomologists. That's quite a word! What do entomologists do?

BETH: Um, I forget, but . . .

ELLEN D.: But some of you have heard that word? It is a word for a special kind of scientist.

DEBBIE: I forget what they're called, but there's a kind of scientist that studies bugs.

ELLEN D.: That's it! Entomologists study insects.

DEBBIE: They have a different name.

ELLEN D.: Hmm. We had a different name last year for the scientists that study birds. Anybody remember that one? (*There are a few negative head shakes and some blank looks.*) Here's how it looks. (*I write* ornithologists *on the chart and make a mental note that this once familiar term did not "stick," which perhaps argues against devoting too much time to scientific vocabulary.*)

DEBBIE: Oh, yes!

ELLEN D.: Okay. Beth says that there are lots of different kinds of scientists, and that they do research. What do you mean, *research*?

BETH: Research about what, you know . . .

LIZ: The things they study.

TERRY: Like if they're an entomologist, they do research on bugs.

ELLEN D.: Other ideas about what scientists do?

DEBBIE: Their research is trying to figure out more about the subject that they're studying.

ELLEN D.: Yes. That's a good way to put it. (*I write Debbie's idea on a chart.*) So things like insects are examples of . . .

DEBBIE: What they're studying.

ELLEN D.: Any other ideas about what scientists do?

SUSAN: There's a group of scientists that are on TV a lot. They're studying birds that are extinct, that are getting extinct. And they're trying to find ways to help them. Like they're feeding them with puppets that look like what their mothers look like.

ELLEN D.: So some scientists are not only studying about something and trying to find out more about a subject, they're actually trying to change something or do something.

Susan shares some information about a breeding program to save a threatened species from extinction. I inquire about the term *extinct*, and she explains it means "that there's no more left, like dinosaurs." Joan then returns to considering types of scientists, noting that some study the ocean.

"Marine biologists!" Lisa chimes in.

I am ready to move on, but the girls are enjoying this line of thought. Within a few minutes they have identified many kinds of scientists (including "rocktologists") and noted that "they all have -*ogist* at the end of their names." I remind the girls of some other common ground that Beth mentioned earlier: scientists do research. I ask if there is anything else they do.

SUSAN: Well, they're working to try and find out more about something. So they can help prevent it, or make it better. They have different reasons they want to find out, but in their research they're all trying to find out more about something.

ELLEN D.: What are the things that they do to find out? Jennifer, can you think of one?

JENNIFER: Well, if they wanted to find out more about a certain kind of bird, they'd watch it.

ELLEN D.: They'd watch it.

KATHY: They'd do tests.

ELLEN D.: They'd do tests. The kind where you have to spell a word right?

KATHY: No! The kind where you have to do different tests on the subject, um, like . . .

ELLEN D.: It's a hard thing to describe.

KATHY: Like designing a test to figure out more.

LISA: Observations.

SUSAN (*offering an example to clarify*): A scientist was trying to find out how poisonous a certain kind of fish was so she put a plastic bag over some coral. Pretty soon all the other fish in the bag were dead from the poison. (*Unlike the five-year-olds, Susan can relate cause and effect and is aware that scientists sometimes manipulate the world in order to answer a specific question.*)

ELLEN D.: Wow! What do you call the thing she did to find out?

SUSAN: A test.

ELLEN D.: Yes, it's a test. And there's another word for it, too.

MARJIE: Experiment.

I sum up: scientists try to find out more about the things that they care about by watching and doing tests. Debbie adds that they have special places, such as sanctuaries, where they work.

Moving On to Observing

I bring out Checkers, the school guinea pig, and tell the girls they will start their own science work by observing him. Though he is a familiar creature (especially to Beth, who cared for him over the summer), these girls are animal lovers and they are charmed to see him.

ELLEN D. (*recognizing their expertise*): Now, I know that some of you have already spent a *lot* of time with Checkers! For instance, I know that Beth has noticed lots of things about him. (*Beth nods vigorously.*) What's something you notice when you observe him right now?

DEBBIE: His hair looks coarse.

ELLEN D.: Coarse-looking hair.

SUSAN: He squeaks a lot.

ELLEN D.: A lot! I notice Debbie did something. She was very careful about the words she used to report her observation. Debbie said that this guinea pig's fur *looks* coarse. Scientists need to be very careful with their words. How come?

BETH: Well, Debbie said it looks coarse.

DEBBIE: I don't *know*.

SUSAN: She didn't touch it yet so she doesn't know for sure. (*The children laugh as the guinea pig chews on the bars of his cage and squeaks.*)

MARJIE: He chews his bars!

BETH: His eyes are red.

ELLEN D.: What would happen if scientists weren't so careful with their words? If Debbie said his hair *is* coarse?

SUSAN: Well, if it was soft, then she'd say something she didn't really mean.

ELLEN D.: That's right. So scientists are trying to report just what they did notice.

DEBBIE (*laughing as she watches the guinea pig nibbling*): He looks like a dog!

ELLEN D.: What can you see when he does all that funny chewing?

LIZ: He doesn't use his teeth.

ELLEN D.: What are his teeth like? Can you get a good look at them?

BETH: The front teeth are *very* big. (*She demonstrates, baring her incisors.*)

SUSAN: They're like beaver's teeth.

ELLEN D. (*nodding*): Like beaver's teeth.

BETH: Something I noticed a long time ago is they have four toes on the front feet and three on the back.

ELLEN D.: Do you want to show people that? (*Beth carries the guinea pig from girl to girl.*)

ELLEN D.: What about us? What do we have?

JOAN: Same—five fingers, five toes.

ELLEN D.: What about some other animals, like dogs?

SEVERAL GIRLS: I don't know.

JOAN: The same, I think.

DEBBIE: Haven't they got four?

LISA: But some dogs have a little toe, a dewclaw.

ELLEN D.: I was surprised when I first noticed the guinea pig's toes. I had just assumed there would be the same number, front and back. Debbie talked before about his fur. Would anyone like the chance to hold him for a minute to see how he feels? (*Children nod.*)

BETH (*picking up the guina pig*): He feels soft!

The girls gently pass the guinea pig around their circle. Kathy, who is mildly allergic to fur, takes a look but doesn't touch. The girls giggle as Checkers nibbles Jennifer's hair.

DEBBIE: He's curious.

ELLEN D. (*pressing them to distinguish between their observations and inferences*): Curious. What do you see that makes you think so?

DEBBIE: He's sniffing around.

SUSAN: And squeaking.

BETH: I noticed this about mine—when you pet her in different places she makes different kinds of squeaks.

ELLEN D.: Really?

BETH: Like when you pet her down her back she goes *purrrr*, but when you touch her around the neck she goes *weak weak, weak weak.*

ELLEN D.: So she makes different sounds in different kinds of situations. (*Although my summary does not accurately express Beth's observation, she has identified an area for further study. I make a mental note to return to it at some point.*)

SUSAN: This guinea pig is squeaking like mad!

ELLEN D.: I wonder if it is disturbing to him to be passed around a circle of giants? I notice how gently you are touching him, and how still you are sitting. You're doing what you can to make this meeting safe for him.

LIZ: My rabbit was that size when I got her.

ELLEN D.: Little! While the last turns are being taken, you can get to work on your own observations. Remember these worksheets? (*These children have used similar forms in previous school years.*)

CHILDREN: Yes.

ELLEN D.: Here's a place for . . .

BETH: Name and date.

JOAN: And what you're observing.

ELLEN D.: What materials do you need to get to help with this work?

GIRLS: Clipboards. Pencils. We have colored pencils, too.

ELLEN D.: Great! I'm going to slide his cage out into the middle of the circle so you can see him from all sides.

The girls collect materials and resettle themselves. Several begin drawing immediately, looking frequently from guinea pig to paper. Others watch the guinea pig. Susan notices his water bottle is low, removes it from the cage and refills it. Observation, drawing, and discussion continue. The general tone is at once relaxed and focused.

DEBBIE: It's eating the cage again!

ELLEN D.: You get a really good look at the mouth when he does that.

BETH: Guinea pigs' eyes are really red.

ELLEN D.: Red?

BETH: Now they look black, but if you see them in the light, then they're really red.

ELLEN D.: So it depends on the light, how they look?

BETH: Yeah. I read about them in a book. Now they look black, but in the light, they're red.

There is more we might understand about this idea. Perhaps it, too, will be one we return to. For now, the children continue to observe and talk. The guinea pig returns to drink from his bottle from time to time.

BETH: He's still drinking! Look at his mouth!

ELLEN D.: That would be hard to describe. How would you talk about it?

BETH: He sticks his tongue up in there and kind of pulls the water down.

DEBBIE: No, he pushes on the ball.

ELLEN D.: What can you see him doing with his jaw when he drinks?

GIRLS: Biting.

LISA (*erasing*): I can't make the legs!

ELLEN D.: The legs are hard to draw.

DEBBIE: Very. I can never get proportions right.

ELLEN D.: And a guinea pig has kind of unusual proportions. How long are his legs?

DEBBIE: Very short compared to his body. At least it looks like that. But you know, a rabbit's tail just looks like a little puff. But if you stretch it all the way out, it's this long (*holds up thumb and finger to show*).

KATHY: Does he have a tail?

BETH: No.

ELLEN D.: Do you want to see? I know you can't touch him, but if Beth holds him up you'll be able to get a good look. (*All of the girls stop their drawing to look.*)

BETH: You can feel something like a—it's not really a tail—bumps, like maybe a backbone.

ELLEN D.: It's an interesting question. Most furry animals I've seen *do* have a tail.

In retrospect, I wish I'd had the girls feel the guinea pig's legs to check their length, too. It would have allowed Debbie to confirm her idea that they were short.

What's Taking Place

The girls observed and drew for a total of about twenty-five minutes. During that time, they talked informally about the guinea pig's behavior, one another's drawings, and information gleaned from books or other experiences with animals. They were at once amused by the guinea pig's antics and serious about studying him. Questions emerged, and some of these were investigated on the spot. At the end of the period, most of the girls appeared satisfied and handed in their records. (Two are shown in Figure 3–3.) Several others felt they hadn't finished what they set out to do and asked to continue later in the day.

For this age group, as with the younger children, my availability was important. I tried to recognize and respond to children's observations, demonstrate ways of observing, and resolve difficulties as they arose. Thoughtful questions or comments from a teacher can prompt children to clarify, analyze, extend, or reconsider, and help children learn ways of working that are both scientific and fun.

Figure 3–3a Guinea pig by ten-year-old girl

Figure 3–3b Guinea pig by Beth, age 10

A simple activity such as observing a class pet provides children with a base on which to build fundamental concepts about the characteristics of oraganisms and how they interact with their environments. According to Content Standard C, Children in grades K–4 need such opportunities (NRC 1996, 129).

Science in School

When Timmy noticed that the guinea pig "took a squeak," when Rachel counted his toes, and when Susan compared his teeth to those of a beaver, they were doing what any curious children might do in the presence of such a creature. Why, then, make a point of linking their activity to science? Why frame guinea pig watching (or experimenting with acids and bases, for that matter) as "doing what scientists do"?

One reason is that some children find it exciting to compare themselves to scientists. For them, the parallel heightens the feeling that they are involved in something important and doing "real work." I hope it also suggests that science is something that *everyone* can do and understand, for I aim to counter the notion that science is for "brains" and that most of us aren't capable of making discoveries or understanding scientific ideas.

Introducing science in the manner described above can also establish an orderly, purposeful "climate." This can be reassuring to teachers and children alike. When the classroom feels "under control," teachers are able to devote their attention to children's observations and questions.

In addition, classrooms are nested within larger institutions, and the way we structure science activities must take that into account. Many teachers are expected to link particular projects or periods of the day to major subject areas. This is part of how we demonstrate "accountability" and facilitate curricular conversations with parents and colleagues. Helping children understand which part of their schoolwork is called "science" becomes important under these circumstances. Even more important is to help children understand that science is a human endeavor (see Content Standard G, NRC 1996, 141, 170–71). Discussing what scientists do is a way to do so.

Explicit discussions of science may also be helpful to children who will eventually take tests or read texts that assume familiarity with the terms and activities that are associated with the discipline. If children are in fact observing, designing experiments, or engaging in other scientific processes, they can begin to match the traditional vocabulary of science to these experiences. Science is not just for "brains," nor should it be the exclusive province of people who can "talk the talk." However, in a culture where tests and texts are laden with specialized vocabulary, introducing children to the language of science can be empowering.

That said, we do well to realize that some children may not readily understand distinctions among the familiar academic disciplines. One group of second-graders I taught could not hang on to the definition of "social studies" I repeatedly offered, and they saw little connection between their own efforts to understand why some objects float and the things they thought scientists would do. The particulars of their studies fascinated them, but my efforts to link these to broad subject areas were confusing.

Are there drawbacks to asking children to consider what scientists do before letting them approach an organism or phenomenon? Alex, the five-year-old who told me that scientists make "weird paintings," suggests one. Young children, as well as older children who have not been exposed to professional or school science, lack experience they can draw on when formulating an answer. They may have little to contribute to a discussion or make statements that are not quite what we hope to hear. It is important that science lessons do not become games in which children must guess what teachers have in mind. If things seem headed in this direction, we can offer an age-appropriate definition of science instead of belaboring the question. It is also important to consider how much emphasis on speaking and listening is productive for particular children or classes. For children who are not fluent in the language of instruction, and for those who have difficulty processing language or paying attention during discussions, it is important to keep science from becoming too much talk.

4 *Another Way to Begin*

Chapter 3 discusses how to initiate science work by defining it and using children's notions about what scientists do, together with your own ideas, to frame some basic activities focused on observing, describing, and recording information. Another way to proceed puts these things aside and emphasizes the specific topic of study. You pose a problem or present some materials and essentially say, "Here. Pay attention to this!" without drawing a parallel between professional science and the work you want children to do. Any advance directives are specific to the materials or activity at hand.

Teachers who begin with more general directives or who explicitly link children's work to science early in the year may gradually change course as the weeks go by and comfortable routines are established. At whatever point you try this approach, the following example shows how it might look.

Getting to Know Crickets

I called six second-graders to a table at the back of the room. I explained that we were going to study crickets and handed each child a cricket caged in a clear plastic punch cup. A chorus of excited exclamations ensued.

"Oooh!"

"Cool!"

"Chop chop chop chop . . ."

"They won't bite."

"We had this little cricket that bites."

"How many crickets are there?"

"Do we each get a cricket?"

"Are we gonna take care of them?"

"You each have one cricket," I acknowledged, "and the first thing to do is just look at it and see what you notice about it."

"I'm going to draw mine!" Jerome announced. He grabbed some paper and began a picture. (I had set colored pencils and paper out on the table, imagining we might use them later on. Their presence, however, suggests an approach.)

While Jerome drew, other children were preoccupied with matters of ownership.

"Can we just write our initials on the top of the cup, so we know which one is ours?"

I said initialing was fine but that the punch cups were only temporary housing. "See that big cage by the sink? That's where we're going to put all the crickets most of the time." My announcement was greeted with dismay.

"How do we know where ours is?"

"We need sections!"

"I want to leave mine in my own cup."

I had hoped that the children would take an immediate interest in the crickets' appearance and behavior, but it seemed that keeping track of "their own" was a high priority. I pressed the children to think of additional ways they could be sure, later on, of a cricket's identity.

"Well," Mei offered, "I could tie a little ribbon around its antenna."

"Hey!" interrupted Keith. "Hey! I notice something about him! I already have a way! 'Cause his back—"

I ask Keith to wait while I call the group's attention to his announcement.

ELLEN D.: Keith thinks he's going to be able to tell his cricket without any compartments or any marks. How do you think you're going to know that cricket again?

KEITH: Because his whiskers, one of his whiskers is shorter and his tail is very short.

SYLVIE: That's the same with me, Keith! One of my whiskers is shorter.

ELLEN D.: Put your two crickets close together. Keith, you can go over and sit by Sylvie for a moment. See if there's anything else that would set those two apart.

SYLVIE: Okay, Keith. I wanna look at yours.

KEITH: Hold it! Your cricket's tail is long.

JASMINE: Sylvie! Yours is bigger than Keith's.

Already the children have noticed a number of features shared by crickets in general as well as a range of individual variation.

Keith and Sylvie look closely at their two crickets and continue to comment on their appearance. Sylvie sees a little red spot on her cricket's leg, and Mei says, "Mine has one, too."

While Jerome continues to draw, the other children peer into their punch cups, offering rapid-fire reactions, problems, plans, and observations.

"Cute!"

"They stink!"

"I'm gonna write every little detail."

Several girls remain concerned because their crickets don't have unique markings. How will they know whose is whose once they are combined in the big cage?

"Does it matter if the crickets get mixed up or not?" I ask, wondering at the intensity of their concern. "What do you think?"

"No."

"Yes!"

Lillian is unequivocal. "I want this cricket each time!"

Sylvie, who has by now taken up paper and pencil, reasons, "Well, if I don't finish my drawing I'll need the same cricket!"

Lillian makes no attempt to relate her wish to anything beyond the personal. "This cricket is a cute little guy so I want this one each time."

Other children feel similarly: "I want this one." "I like this one." "Mine is a very important cricket!"

As they assert their claims, they continue to observe.

"Hey! This one has little pink spots by its knees!"

"It's a girl!" rings out in response. While clearly said in jest, the comment sparks serious thought.

"How can you tell if it's a boy or a girl?" Sylvie wonders.

I keep track of the questions that surface. There isn't any need to answer: later, when the initial flurry of activity settles down a bit, the children can devise ways to investigate.

Keith, still looking intently at his cricket, calls my attention to another feature. "I noticed that on the very tippy tip of its back leg, on every leg, there's two little things like that." Keith sketches two tiny hooked lines, like little claws.

Lillian has turned her cricket over for a better look. When she rights the container, the cricket remains clinging to the top, upside down. "Let go!" she scolds.

"How do they do that?" another child wonders aloud.

Figure 4–1 **Drawings of crickets**

Several children repeat the experiment, turning their cups upside down and back again. The crickets slide down the plastic sides, then, like Lillian's, hang on to the lids—even after the cups are righted.

"How do their legs stick?"

"You guys, look at this!"

"How do their legs stick to the top?"

"Oh, look at mine! Look at mine!"

"I'm going to do that again!"

A new question emerges from the general commotion: "Do crickets lay eggs?"

I'm not sure who has raised it. Before I can inquire, Lillian announces, "I was the first one to discover they can stick to the top!"

"Mine can't!" Keith pouts. He has inverted his cup so quickly, the cricket hasn't been able to catch hold of the lid.

Jerome, who has remained a little apart from the fray, summons my attention. "They have these, like, little muscles on their legs," he notes.

"Where do you see that?"

"If you look with the magnifying glass, their legs sort of puff up at a certain part . . . and it sort of looks like muscles."

I take a look, then return my attention to the other children, who are continuing their fascination with the upside-down crickets.

"It sticks to the top!" someone exclaims.

"How do you suppose it can do that?" I ask.

"I have no idea!" she replies.

Keith, however, does have an idea. He relates an earlier observation to this novel ability. "They have little dogchams," he asserts. "They have little hookiedoos."

"What's a hookiedoo?" asks Sylvie.

Remembering the sketch Keith had made of two clawlike structures, I ask if he he is talking about those.

Lillian answers for him, "Yeah. Little hookiedoos."

"Yeah," Keith concurs.

I suggest that Lillian and Keith try to figure out whether they are both referring to the same structure. Keith, who by now has a more elaborate drawing underway, points out the "hookiedoos" on his new picture. Lillian concludes that they have, indeed, recognized the same feature (see Figure 4–2).

"Lillian," I ask, "what happens with the hookiedoos when the cricket goes upside down?"

"They just, like, grab onto the top," she explains.

Hanging upside down was not the only strange thing the crickets did during this introductory session. Mei was the first to notice another surprising behavior.

MEI: He's chewing on his antenna! He's chewing on his antenna!

ELLEN D.: Chewing on its antenna!

MEI: He was. Hey! He's chewing on his antenna again!

ELLEN D.: Yours does a lot of that, Mei!

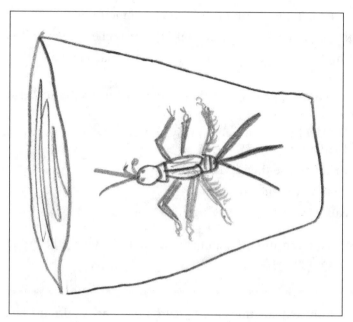

Figure 4–2 Keith and the child who drew this cricket both noticed tiny claws on its feet

MEI: Well, I think I can tell. (*Mei is still seeking a way to distinguish her cricket from others, and thinks perhaps the antenna chewing is unique. She seeks confirmation from the other children.*) Does yours chew on its antenna?

SYLVIE (*directing the question to her cricket*): Do you chew on your antenna?

MEI (*to Keith*): Does yours ever chew on its antenna?

KEITH: Nope.

MEI (*to Sylvie and Jerome*): Did yours ever chew on its antenna?

SYLVIE: How should we know? We just got them a minute!

MEI: No, but has it been at all?

SYLVIE: No.

ELLEN D. (*hoping to cast doubt on any conclusions based on such slim evidence*): What do you think about that? Do you think it means it never does it, if it hasn't done it yet?

MEI: That means that we can tell ours apart, because mine's the only one that's chewing on its antenna. Well, maybe it's hungry.

ELLEN D.: Jasmine? What do you think about Mei's idea?

JASMINE: I don't know. But I think I notice something.

LILLIAN: It's chewing on its antenna! Mine was chewing on its antenna!

MEI: Uh-oh! Hers was chewing on its antenna. It seems like they're hungry.

LILLIAN: What happens when they chew on their antennas? I have no idea!

ELLEN D.: Mei has an idea about maybe why they do it. Do you want to tell Lillian that idea?

MEI: I think maybe they're a little hungry.

LILLIAN: Or maybe they have an itch.

MEI: Yeah. Maybe they're having an itch on their antennae.

Two children discuss another possibility. "Maybe they're cleaning themselves," one says.

Scientific explanations are based on evidence and must be revised as new evidence comes to light. Children begin to realize this as they try to reconcile observations with initial ideas. When Lillian spotted a cricket "chewing" its antenna, Mei realized that this behavior was not unique to her own cricket. She also considered different interpretations: perhaps the crickets were hungry, itchy, or cleaning themselves. Evidence and explanation are fundamental concepts described in the *Standards* (NRC 1996, 113–17).

While some children monitor the antenna chewing, others attend to a feature noticed earlier.

"They have little red spots on their legs."

"Oh yeah!"

"So does mine."

"Mine, too."

"Both of the back legs."

"All of them have red spots on their legs."

The session continues in this lively, nonlinear fashion. Observations are made, explanations proposed, and questions raised. Topics are discussed, dropped, then brought up later as if for the first time. What do crickets eat? How do they go to the bathroom? Why do they chew on their antennae? Some children complete detailed drawings; others barely apply pencil to paper. Several work together in loose collaboration, comparing observations and critiquing one another's ideas. Jerome remains a bit detached from the group. The problem that motivated much of the children's work remains only partly solved. How can you—*for sure*—tell your very own cricket from the rest?

Though little is settled, recess, lunch, and other matters demand our attention. I have the children wrap up their work. I make sure that crickets are caged and papers stored for future reference. However, I make no attempt at closure in the sense of reviewing facts learned or principles discovered. This was not a "lesson" so much as a beginning. Another day, we will pick up where we left off.

What Took Place

What did the children make of their experience? Before the close of the school day, various second-graders reported on their activities at a brief whole-class meeting. Jasmine described what had gone on at the back table by saying, "We were getting to know the crickets." She did not refer to her work as science, nor did any child in her group use that term at any point. They were focused on the specifics of the enterprise: particular crickets, their odd behavior, and which colored pencil would best illustrate the pink spots on the legs.

I, too, noted these specifics. From my vantage point as teacher, I also saw many elements of good elementary science in what the children spontaneously did. They noticed, compared, explained, raised questions, and made records. They considered alternate hypotheses. The groundwork for future investigations was laid, and the interest needed to fuel them was aroused. One not-so-scientific priority was the desire to possess a particular cricket. This impulse is common among young children and rarely threatens investigations of the kind I like to see. In this case, it encouraged the close attention to the crickets that I was hoping for.

My role during this first session was largely to bring the children and crickets into proximity. I also encouraged children to pay attention to what the crickets looked like and were doing through my questions and by displaying my own interest. If such attention can be maintained—for several class periods, weeks, or even months—the children are bound to notice many odd and intriguing things that will help them piece together what crickets can do and how they live. The appearance of a shed skin in the cricket cage a few days into this study raised questions about how crickets grow and change. Some of these were answered over time as the crickets matured. Sylvie eventually determined that her cricket was a "girl" through a combination of close observation, reading, and reasoning. The "dot" she noticed at the end of its abdomen, which lengthened

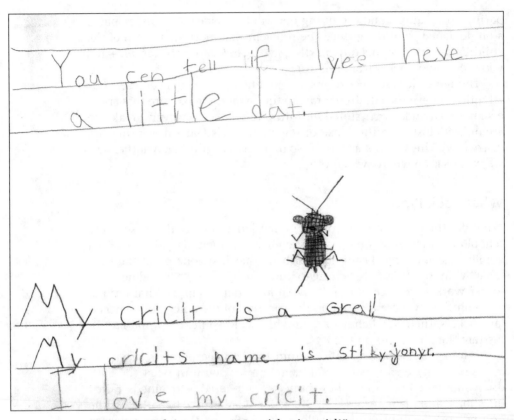

You cen tell if lyee heve a little dat.

My cricit is a gral!

My cricits name is stikyjonyr.

I love my cricit.

Figure 4–3 **Sylvie reports, "My cricket is a girl!"**

slightly when the cricket molted, seemed to match the ovipositors, or egg-laying structures, depicted in books (Figure 4–3).

Sylvie's curiosity about the sex of her cricket and the dot on its abdomen sparked an investigation that deepened her understanding of a fundamental concept highlighted in the *Standards*: "Each plant or animal has different structures that serve different functions in growth, survival, and reproduction" (NRC 1996, 129).

What I like about working in this organic way is that the subject matter—whatever it is—gets full and immediate attention, and children, unhampered by definitions or rules about how to proceed, often approach the activity with energy and self-direction, spontaneously initiating many of the investigations I would steer them toward if I were controlling the activity to a greater degree. They also suggest avenues of exploration I haven't thought of. Children who find it difficult to listen for long periods or who are new to the language of instruction may especially appreciate moving quickly to small-group or independent work without a lengthy meeting first.

Teachers often worry about how they will manage to address each of the standards that have been outlined by the National Research Council. However, instances like the one described above promote many at once. Important aspects of several teaching standards were addressed when I set aside time and space in which children could work, introduced the crickets, facilitated the experience, and helped children attend to one another's ideas. Children raised questions, sought answers, and learned about the characteristics of a particular organism (Content Standards A and C). The crickets set the stage for developing the idea that form is related to function (a unifying concept in science and in the *Standards*). Keith discovered two little "dogchams," or "hookiedoos," on the tip of his cricket's legs, while other children noticed that their crickets could hang upside down from the cup lids. Further investigation revealed a relationship (NRC 1996, 115–29).

Learning to Look

Over the course of the year, I want to see children involved in all kinds of science activity—collecting, classifying, hypothesizing, experimenting, and so forth—but initially I emphasize observation. Making observations is at the heart of scientific inquiry. We simply can't raise questions and design investigations about things we haven't noticed in the first place. Yet it is easy to be heedless as we go about our daily routines. We miss the obvious, see what we expect to see rather than what is actually before us, or dismiss a thing as boring or insignificant without knowing much about it. So, I like to help children cultivate the ability to focus and notice.

Observing an object, plant, or animal is a straightforward way to initiate elementary science. But what to concentrate on? Sometimes I choose an object that relates to a topic we'll study in depth—it could be seeds if we'll be raising plants. The initial observation then serves as an appetizer, a doorway to the longer study. Other times I simply select something that intrigues me and that I think will interest children—perhaps a beautiful shell, a bone, a flower.

Certain things have special appeal for particular age groups. For seven-year-olds—who love tiny worlds—I might choose an insect or a clump of lichen on a log; for five- and six-year-olds, something familiar—a pet or garden vegetable. Older children often enjoy a mystery and appreciate an object that takes some effort to identify. Whatever you choose, asking children to observe it is an invitation to do far more than take a quick look. In this example and those in Chapter 3, children watch animals but also share information and ideas, interpret their observations, identify patterns, react to things that seem funny or surprising, and draw on information from previous experiences. Just as scientists employ many skills simultaneously, children develop a range of abilities and interests at one time.

The Teacher's Role

Whether you begin by considering what scientists do or by diving in and asking children to "get to know" some creature or thing, your availability as they start to look and wonder is important. If the entire class is observing something at the same time, you can circulate through the room. I often start the year this way, gathering many similar specimens so that each child can have one. If I decide to work with fewer children instead, I give the others an assignment they can manage independently. I keep an eye on the whole room, but devote most of my attention to the small group I am launching.

In each of the "beginnings" I've described, I was free from certain duties often associated with teaching science. I did not tell children about the habits or life cycles of animals nor list specific questions for them to answer. I was, however, very busy. In trying to create a climate in which children would become active explorers of the world around them and in which both self-reliance and cooperation would be valued, I worked with deliberation. I watched as children got settled at their work.

In the K–1 class, I noticed that Brian got to work quickly and focused on his observation. And I noticed Neil standing nearby, watching the blocks first, then the other children in his group. I expected that the children would approach the task variously, and I waited to see what this behavior of Neil's meant. Was he wasting time? Doing nothing? Was he distracted or forgetful? Was he learning what to do by watching others work, gaining the confidence to try? I heard Alex ask for reassurance before he began: "Does it go this way? Is here where I put my name?" He wanted to do the work right. By providing the reassurance he needed, I released him to make a start.

My focus was similarly broad as the older children studied their crickets. I took note of how children worked as well as of their particular discoveries and questions. This information serves me as I plan ways to follow up on the experience and extend children's ability to observe and inquire.

5 Building a Culture of Collaboration

In classrooms where children exchange information, observations, and ideas, everyone's thinking gets a push. Children need chances to work together if they are to gain all that is possible from doing science in school. However, opportunity is only the beginning. Simply organizing children into groups does not ensure that they will listen attentively to others, consider new ideas thoughtfully, disagree respectfully, include newcomers with generosity, or accommodate the range of needs and paces they encounter. What can teachers do to cultivate these valuable abilities?

One option is to teach the skills and practices they require. Traveling in a herd of twenty or so—the norm in elementary classrooms—challenges teachers and children in many ways. It demands more waiting, better listening, louder speaking, and a greater tolerance for others than do many situations in which children find themselves. Consequently, I teach etiquette along with science and try to structure activities to encourage courteous interaction.

This takes patient deliberation and, of course, time. I'll confess I can feel a bit grudging about the time: my real interest is science, not manners, and there are never enough minutes in a day to fit everything in. However, I know I won't end up with the kind of science I want if I don't also attend to the classroom climate.

Attending to One Another: Minding Our Manners

Science investigations often stretch out over weeks or even months. During this time, I like to alternate periods of independent or small-group work with "science meetings." These meetings are a forum for sharing information, discussing questions, and establishing what to do next. They also allow me to introduce ways of demonstrating attention and responding to others. My hope is that teaching these "meeting manners" will facilitate kindly exchange in this tightly structured setting and serve children in other situations as well.

Early Science Meetings

In the first example, the children who observed the guinea pig in Chapter 3 gather with their class for a formal introduction to the meeting process. As my comments reveal, manners are much on my mind. While I don't ignore the discoveries children have made, a major aim is getting children to behave in ways that assure classmates it is safe to join in.

I signal for children to come to our meeting area and, with a little coaching, they arrange themselves in a circle. I tell them that scientists sometimes gather at meetings and ask why this might be so. Sara volunteers that they might want to share their work, and Timmy says, "To find out more stuff." I say that our science meetings will be for the same things: sharing work and hearing from others.

I decide to let children rehearse these activities by having Amy tell about her observations of the guinea pig. I have collected the children's worksheets before the meeting, and I hand Amy hers as she crosses the circle and stands next to me.

Ellen D.: An important job for the scientist sharing is to show her picture so that everyone in the circle can see it. Scientists can learn by studying each other's drawings. Amy, can you find a way to stand right here but show your picture to everyone? (*Amy holds up her picture, turning so that everyone has a chance to see it.*)

Tracy: I didn't see.

Ellen D.: We do want everyone to be able to see! But it's easy when you're showing your work to miss someone. If you don't get a good look, what can you do?

Tracy: Ask her to see it.

Ellen D.: Yes. Show me how you can get Amy's attention. (*Tracy raises her hand.*) Yes, it's so important to raise your hand! Amy could be feeling nervous up here, showing her work. And she has an important job to be concentrating on. What could happen if everyone just shouts out, "I can't see"?

Rachel: She might feel bad.

Danny: She could get mixed up.

Ellen D.: Right. So a way we can take care of Amy while she's sharing her work is to watch her show her picture, then raise our hands if we need a better look at it. Amy has another job at this meeting. She can say something she noticed about the guinea pig, or she can read what she wrote. Amy, which would you like to do?

AMY: Say it.

ELLEN D.: Fine. Find a really big voice to say it with so everyone can hear.

AMY: I noticed he has toenails.

ELLEN D.: Amy has shown us what the job of the scientist sharing is. Who knows what the job of the other scientists at the meeting is?

RANDY: To listen.

ELLEN D.: Yes. The other scientists will listen, so they can learn more. And how will Amy know you are listening? (*Some kids sit up straight and look at Amy.*) I see John doing something. John, what are you doing that shows Amy you're listening?

JOHN: Not talking.

ELLEN D.: I noticed that. What were you doing instead?

JOHN: Looking at her.

ELLEN D.: Yes. Looking at Amy. And holding your body—

JOHN: Still!

While children can indeed pay attention when they are wiggling, fidgeting, or lying down, sitting reasonably still may make it easier for the facilitator, person sharing, or another member of the group to focus, so I have called attention to John's effort.

ELLEN D.: So the other scientists at the meeting are sitting still and looking at Amy's picture and listening when she talks. They also have another important job. They will be thinking about her work— thinking whether they understand it, whether they have a question or comment for her. Scientists want other people to understand their work. The comments we make show Amy what we understand. When you see Amy's picture, what's a comment you might have?

KATHLEEN: I like it.

Kathleen's compliment is kindly meant. However, I want this meeting to become a forum for exchanging information about a topic rather than for offering general praise or acknowledging friends, so I ask Kathleen to explain her judgment a bit.

ELLEN D.: You think Amy did a good job drawing the guinea pig? (*Kathleen nods.*) How do you know if a science drawing is a good one?

KATHLEEN: If it looks like the real one.

ELLEN D.: So scientists try to make their illustrations realistic. (*Realism is only one worthwhile standard to aim for, but I let the others go. Kathleen has linked Amy's drawing to the guinea pig, and for now, that is enough.*) What did Amy show in her guinea pig that the real guinea pig has?

KATHLEEN: Fur!

ELLEN D.: What color did she make the fur?

SARA: Brown and white.

ELLEN D.: So a comment for Amy could be, "I notice you showed the guinea pig's brown-and-white fur," or "You drew fur like on the real guinea pig." Who's ready to practice a comment?

BRIAN: I notice you made his eyes.

MARGARET: I notice you put the water bottle in.

NICKY: I like your picture. You made his nose!

ELLEN D.: Those are all helpful comments for Amy. You might also have a question for Amy about her work. Maybe you notice she told about the guinea pig's toes and you want to know how she found out how many he had. How could you ask that?

JOHN: How did you find out how much toes he has?

AMY: I counted when Ellen was holding him.

ELLEN D.: You can also ask a question if you don't understand something, or if you couldn't hear or see. Anybody want to try?

ROBBIE: I didn't hear. Can you read it again?

ELLEN D.: Could I say, "I don't like your drawing," or, "You forgot to show the ears?"

CHILDREN: No.

ELLEN D.: How come?

LISA: That would hurt someone's feelings.

ELLEN D.: What if you were looking at my picture, and I really did forget the ears?

RANDY: Just—say nothing.

ELLEN D.: That would be taking good care of my feelings. Could you still make a comment, even if I forgot the ears?

NEIL: Yes.

ELLEN D.: What could you say?

NEIL: You could just say about the other parts.

Admonishing children to "say what is true but not all that is true" can prohibit productive discussion if stressed too firmly. It is important for children to be able to question one another and offer constructive suggestions. At this early point in the school year, though, I urge taking tender care with comments. I hope to create a climate in which even the most reticent children will venture a contribution.

This rehearsal took just a few minutes during which Amy demonstrated how to show a picture so others can see it and also shared some information about the guinea pig. Her classmates listened and thought about what she presented. I expected them to respond, but I also set some boundaries. Children could react to what they had heard or seen, ask questions to get more information, or speak up if they were confused, couldn't see, or couldn't hear. Potentially hurtful criticism was to be avoided.

Afterward, I offered Amy a "real" turn to share, one uninterrupted by my directions and comments.

Danny went next. As he stood to speak, a few quiet conversations started up around the circle. Tracy began adjusting the Velcro on her sneakers, and Randy shifted from sitting down to lying down.

ELLEN D. (*to Danny*): I see you are ready to begin. You'll know everyone is ready to listen when you see that everyone is sitting still and looking at you. (*Danny looks around the circle of children. Randy sits up, Tracy sticks her Velcro in place, and Danny holds out his picture for everyone to see. A similar one appears in Chapter 6.*) What's something you noticed when you looked at the guinea pig, Danny?

DANNY: He squeaks.

ELLEN D.: When you're ready, you can ask for questions or comments. (*I put children themselves in charge of questions and comments whenever possible. Even very young children can direct a portion of the meeting in this way.*)

DANNY: I'm ready for questions and comments. Joel?

JOEL: What's that part in the middle?

DANNY: Here? (*Joel nods.*) That's his heart. It's on the inside. Kate?

KATE: I can't see. (*Danny turns his paper and points out the heart to Kate.*)

DANNY: Laurie?

LAURIE: I like your picture, and he can squeak loud!

DANNY: I know!

ELLEN D.: One more question or comment for Danny.

DANNY: Michael?

MICHAEL: I notice you made his eyes.

Other children longed for a turn, but wiggles and whispers convinced me that it was time to move on. I listed on chart paper the discoveries that Amy and Danny reported and asked the rest of the class for additions. The meeting grew lively, and the paper quickly filled. It would serve as a point of departure another time.

With older children, the basic pattern of sharing followed by questions and comments still works well at early science meetings. Those who are familiar with this classroom structure will need little direction. Others, regardless of age, may benefit from reviewing ways to participate politely. In the following example, Marion, age eight, begins.

MARION: I looked at a feather. (*Reading from her worksheet.*) "The bottom has white fluffy things. The shaft looks like plastic. One side is darker than the other side. The shaft gets smaller when it goes up. The feather looks like a paddle. On one side it has a white outline but on the other side it doesn't have the outline." Questions or comments?

ANDREA: I like your picture. It's realistic.

CHIP: You showed all of the different colors.

Figure 5–1 Guinea pig by girl, age six

Figure 5–2   Drawing of a feather

ELLEN D.: Can you tell people again, Marion, that word for this plasticky part?

MARION: The shaft.

ELLEN D.: The shaft.

JAY: I saw that feather and I think your picture really looks like it.

As before, etiquette here is geared toward:

- Making sure everyone can see and hear
- Ensuring that all feel comfortable enough to contribute
- Encouraging children to attend closely to one another, think about what they see and hear, and ask questions if they don't understand

---

The *Standards* urge a shift in classroom communication, emphasizing "public communication of student ideas and work to classmates" over private conversations between a student and teacher. Teachers promote this shift by structuring and guiding student-to-student dialog about questions, ideas, and findings (NRC 1996, 36, 113). Professional scientists share information about their investigations so that others can repeat and extend them. Science meetings involve children in similar activity.

A Simple, Predictable Environment

In early science meetings, interaction should be structured, formal, and slow-paced. This creates a predictable routine that young children, especially, crave. After two or three such meetings, even five-year-olds know what to count on. Energy that might otherwise be spent trying to discern the teacher's expectations or figure out how to "have a say" can be directed to thinking about the topic at hand. Children at seven and eight can not only take part in such a meeting, they can run it.

Ultimately, I want science meetings to be lively arenas in which children grapple with difficult problems, share uncertainties, discuss the relative merits of different explanations, and generate a kind of collective excitement about the phenomena being studied. Although the format I have outlined may seem inconsistent with that goal, I believe that forums with a reliable structure can provide both teacher and children with great freedom. As Lucy Calkins (1986) writes:

> I have finally realized that the most creative environments in our society are not the kaleidoscopic environments in which everything is always changing and complex. They are, instead, the predictable and consistent ones: the scholar's library, the researcher's laboratory, the artist's studio. Each of these environments is deliberately kept *predictable* and *simple* because the work at hand and the changing interactions around the work are so unpredictable and complex. (12)

Regularly scheduled science meetings offer children a predictable and simple environment in which to think about shared topics of interest. They also provide opportunities to develop the social skills required for more unpredictable, student-directed, collaborative work. Meetings needn't be limited to sharing previously made observations and receiving a few comments. Teachers and children can use them flexibly to solve problems, plan trips, or define research questions. Over time, teachers can be alert for signs of boredom or frustration that may indicate the structure has become restrictive.

Trying to Find Out

I once visited a second-grade classroom where children were studying pond animals. Bobby, age seven, greeted me with news of recent developments. "Come look at our caddis flies," he urged. I peered into a glass dish housing a number of the insect larvae, each inhabiting a case it had constructed from bits of leaves, reeds, and other aquatic vegetation (see Figure 5–3). "See what they're doing?" Bobby pointed. "Ricky was the first one that noticed that. Now we've all been seeing it."

I watched for a moment. Several of the caddis flies seemed to be bumping into one another, sometimes even climbing atop one another's cases. This was accompanied by lots of up and down movements of their tiny heads. "That is interesting behavior!" I agreed.

Figure 5–3 Caddis fly drawn by eight-year-old boy

Figure 5–4 Children observe caddis fly behavior

"At first we thought they were fighting. That was Kevin's idea, I think. Because it looks like they might be fighting. Then Heather had a different idea. She thought maybe when they climb on top of each other like that, they're mating. But then Jerry said no, these caddis flies are just babies really; the grown-ups look like moths or something. So we decided they probably weren't mating.

"Then I had the theory that one of them is eating the other. Not really eating it, but you know, eating its shell. They move their heads up and down and eat. But now Jenny has a new theory. She thinks they get things from other caddis flies' shells, and they put them on their own shell. We're trying to find out which theory is right."

Bobby's final statement and the easy way in which he credits each classmate's contribution convey the spirit of this enterprise. It is a collaborative effort of the best sort, characterized by real curiosity, a free and collegial exchange of ideas, and thoughtful consideration of a range of explanations. Reasonable doubt has been cast on a particular "theory," but the general tone is one of suspended judgment. A science teacher's dream!

What enables children to work together in this way? It takes more than good manners. It requires a real attachment to the subject matter, inquiring minds, and, when questions surface, the desire to discover real answers—that is, the answers nature would give, if asked. Children have to be more invested in finding out what is really going on than in being "right" or in sticking with first impressions, getting done quickly, or receiving input exclusively from their closest friends.

Scientists must think critically about evidence, and children can learn to do so as well. The *Standards* urge teachers to "encourage and model . . . the curiosity, openness to new ideas, and skepticism that characterize science" (See Teaching Standard B, NRC 1996, 37).

Teachers can't force this to happen. But we can take this stance ourselves. It can shape our work with individual children, and it can also guide our facilitation of science meetings. When it guides mine, I'm conscious of working to get a range of observations, ideas, or explanations "on the table" so they are available to everyone. To further our collective understanding, I ask what many children think and why. Essentially, I try to accomplish through a whole-class discussion what Bobby and his second-grade colleagues did more informally and independently.

Here's an example.

I made several visits to a K–1 classroom where children had been raising monarch caterpillars and watching their transformation into butterflies. Children's observations had sparked many questions. Natalie, for instance, wondered how the whole process began, and whether "they were born from a butterfly or if they were born from a caterpillar." Lee wanted to know if "the age keeps on going with the caterpillar and the butterfly" or whether the time logged as a caterpillar no longer counts after a butterfly emerges from its chrysalis. (While not typically a focus of science units on life cycles, this was important to Lee as he anticipated his own birthday.) Quite a number of children were interested in whether butterflies had bones.

I met with the children to discuss this last question, selecting it over their others because it could be directly explored. I wanted to give children a chance to plan and carry out a simple investigation. When I asked for their thoughts, Emily said, "They do have 'em 'cause they couldn't flap if they didn't have them." Hannah disagreed: "I think that they don't have bones, because their bones might be so strong that they couldn't flap their wings." Already, I could see some of the ideas that informed their decisions: bones were stiff, strong, and related to motion.

I asked if there were any other ideas. Lucas thought that butter-flies lacked bones because butterflies are too skinny to contain them. However, he figured caterpillars *did* have bones because they're fat. Lee wasn't sure this could be true: "Because if that, then how do they lose the bones when—how would they lose their bones inside the cocoon?" (Indeed, what changes, and what remains the same, during metamor-phoses?) Helen didn't think there could be bones in a butterfly, because bones are very heavy and would make the wings too heavy to fly. But Micah thought butterflies could have bones if the bones were "very small and light." Zoe was *sure* they had bones. Otherwise, "their wings would be floppy like this." Zoe demonstrated, limply flapping her hands.

As they puzzle over whether butterflies have bones, young children reveal their growing understanding of form and function, one of the unifying concepts highlighted in the *Standards* (NRC 1996, 115–19).

I might have weighed in with the "right" answer at this point and simply said, "Butterflies don't have bones." Alternatively, I could have read a textbook statement that described insect exoskeletons. But re-sorting to authority in these ways can discourage collaboration. It dis-misses the solid thinking of children like Emily and Zoe, who reasoned that bones lent stiffness to butterfly wings, allowing them to flap. It also discourages the impulse to address scientific questions scientifically, by gathering evidence. So instead I asked the children how they could put their ideas to the test. I told them that I would like to know for sure whether butterflies had bones and wondered how we could find out.

JOSHUA: Well, I really haven't, well, I'm pretty sure this is something you should do if you don't know.

ELLEN D.: Okay, if you don't know what should you do?

JOSHUA: If you see a dead butterfly, just chop it up and see if there's bones.

ELLEN D.: And how would you notice a bone? Do you know what bones look like?

CHILDREN: Yeah!

ELLEN D.: What do they look like?

LESLIE: A white thing.

NATE: They're white and it has a little thing on the end.

ELLEN D.: Okay, so if you chopped up a dead butterfly—

ROSIE: And they're hard! So you can really feel them.

ELLEN D.: Oh. So if it was all full of little hard white things what would you think?

CHILDREN: Bones!

I asked the children for other ideas about how to tell if butterflies had bones, but they returned to Josh's idea instead. Several thought it was worth a try, and one child remembered that there was a dead butterfly under a bush outside the school. I continued to press for more ideas, because I thought there was more than one way to tackle the problem and it would be interesting to see what information another approach revealed. I also wanted to learn more about the understanding of bones and butterflies that led to the original question. Eventually, Annie said, "You can ask a real scientist. Or you could ask someone who knows everything about butterflies." Then Natalie suggested "we find out if we have our bones by hitting—not very hard." She gently slapped her legs to demonstrate, and several classmates followed suit.

"How do you think you could find out about a butterfly or a caterpillar," I asked. "Does that give anybody an idea?" Mandy remembered that her dad "once holded a butterfly" and then he gave it to her to feel the wings and she "felt that there was no bones in there." I took this as a proposal for second experiment: you could feel for bones in a butterfly as well as chop one up to look for them.

The conversation returned briefly to Joshua's idea. Zoe thought that perhaps some butterflies had bones and others didn't, and that you could find out if that was the case by trying Josh's ideas with two different kinds of dead butterflies. Lee pointed out a potential problem: "I think Joshua's idea if you cut them up, you still might not see the bones even if they did have bones because you can see bones on people because they're bigger, but in butterflies they're probably much smaller than our bones, and we might not be able to see them." He seemed to think Josh's idea was worth trying, but that it might be necessary to use a magnifying glass.

There was also some discussion about whether a live or dead butterfly should be used for the feel-for-bones experiment. One child thought a dead one would be best, because a live one would try to get away and you might hurt it. Another thought that "dead butterflies don't have as much muscles." A live one would be "stronger" and, thus, better for the experiment.

I left the group to mull over the options they had generated. Later, their teacher supplied some additional ones, including taking a dead butterfly for an X-ray at a veterinary clinic.

Figure 5–5   **A butterfly**

Examine Assumptions

Getting all the ideas on the table takes time, and some of those that surface will seem odd, incomplete, or unproductive to pursue. It is tempting to take a different path. Sometimes I catch myself trying to steer children's discussion efficiently toward a predetermined conclusion. This conclusion is sometimes based on my own understanding of the subject matter or on my goal of helping students master a particular fact or standard. In these instances, I tend to call on fewer children. When someone delivers the information I'm looking for, I underscore it and move on. I forget to ask why children think as they do, and let assumptions slide by, unexamined. I accept particular information without questioning it because it matches my own notions or goals.

Though I try to be aware of the screens I use to filter my responses to children, I know my success varies. Fortunately, when children have become curious about a subject and have devoted their own time and intelligence to thinking about it, they are often unwilling to settle for less than full partnership. Children who want to collaborate, who believe their ideas and questions have value, and who have the appropriate forum often speak up.

In the following example, I've called together a class of seven- and eight-year-olds for a meeting. The students had been studying crickets for a few days and were ready to share their findings. My aim is to have children pool their observations and highlight any puzzles that might merit investigation.

BEN: I noticed that my cricket has little hairs on its legs.

KIM: Mine does, too. I think they all have that.

BONNIE: They have designs on the wings.

KARIN: Some of the crickets chirp, but not all of them.

MARTY: They have long feelers that look as if they come out of their eyes.

BETH ANN: I noticed that my cricket has two eyes.

JEFF: Some have two little tails on the back, and some have the two little tails with one big tail in the middle.

JACKIE: My cricket has four eyes.

ELLEN D.: Wait a minute: When Beth looked at her cricket, she found two eyes. When Jackie looked, she found four! Did anyone else see eyes on a cricket?

NICKY: Mine had two.

MAUREEN: Mine, too!

GREG: I think that they have lots and lots of eyes—they have a special kind of eyes.

ELLEN D.: Compound eyes?

GREG: That's it.

ELLEN D.: Claudia, you look puzzled.

CLAUDIA: But how do you know where the eyes are? I didn't see any eyes!

DOUGLAS: They're on the head—one on each side—right where the feelers are.

CLAUDIA: But how can you tell those are eyes? Just because our eyes are on our heads doesn't mean a cricket's are!

Claudia was unwilling to make assumptions about crickets based on what she knew about people. Her wise reluctance made me realize my own readiness to make assumptions like this. I, along with Claudia's classmates, had interpreted our observations according to some unarticulated expectations: animals have eyes, and eyes are on heads. I was now forced to consider how I "knew" this. Was it my own close study of crickets, a textbook illustration, or unconscious anthropomorphizing? The first seemed least likely: I could come up with little to support my assumption. I decided it would be a good idea to slow us all down to Claudia's pace and stop taking so much for granted.

ELLEN D.: You have noticed many things about our crickets during the past several days. And it seems there are some questions about the eyes. Some of you counted two, and some of you counted four. Greg thinks there might be lots and lots—that crickets might have a special kind of eyes called "compound eyes." Claudia is wondering how we can be sure the things we are seeing really are the eyes. How will we find out?

KIM: We could look more closely.

ELLEN D.: A closer look might help. And how could you look more closely?

MARTY: Well, we could try the microscope or maybe a magnifying glass.

ELLEN D.: Good ideas. We can try to take a closer look tomorrow. But how will we figure out if the things we think are the eyes really *are* the eyes?

This question, a version of "what are those structures near one end of the cricket," is a good one to get children thinking. It is not necessarily an easy question to answer, especially for young children. In this case, I was unable to think of a way that second- or third-graders might convincingly demonstrate that a particular structure was, or was not, an eye. Children turned instead to books, which proved thoroughly disappointing. Some texts did not mention eyes at all, focusing instead on the interesting habits of particular species. Others offered information about eyes but did not say how that information was obtained. Consulting an entomologist was more helpful, as we could ask what he believed about cricket eyes and also what had convinced him.

In the end, children were able to think about the matter in a fairly sophisticated way. They could sort various "facts" about crickets into categories and associate different degrees of certainty with each. Roughly stated, the categories were:

- Things they felt quite sure about because of what they had seen or because of a concurrence between things they had seen and what others had written or said.

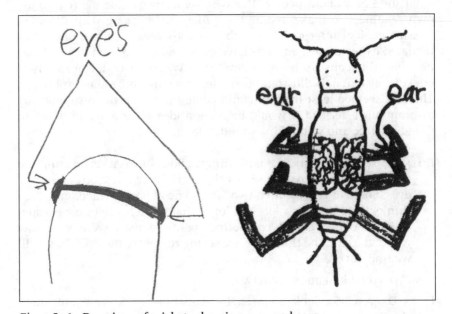

Figure 5–6   Drawings of crickets showing eyes and ears

- Things that might well be true because a seemingly reliable source maintained so, but that we didn't have much firsthand information about.

- Entirely unsettled matters.

The children who are our best allies in establishing a culture of collaboration are the ones, like Claudia, who are unwilling to take things for granted, who listen closely to others and strive to understand what they say, who consider what they hear in light of their own observations, and who will admit that what is obvious to others is not at all clear to them.

Making it possible for children to act in these ways is a crucial task for science teachers.

"But how can you tell those are eyes?" Claudia asked her classmates, seeking evidence to support their claim. Teachers can follow her lead. The *Standards* note that even children in the primary grades "should learn what constitutes evidence and judge the merits or strength of the data and information that will be used to make explanations" (NRC 1996, 122).

Collaborating with Experts

I want to clarify my earlier point that using my status as the teacher or appealing to a text to settle a scientific question could discourage collaboration. I think it is important for teachers to be able to share their own observations and thinking with children, and I continually urge children to consult professional scientists, books, and other sources about the puzzles that surface as they investigate and explore. All of these can inform, enrich, and excite. However, I've come to feel that *how* we encourage children to regard "high-status" individuals, experts, and printed texts also matters. Ideally, children will approach all such sources as Claudia approached her classmates. They will review their own ideas and experiences as they consider information that others present. And they will pose the same questions to experts and authors that Claudia did to her classmates: How do you know? How can you tell?

I haven't always encouraged children to do this. I remember working on an art project with a group of five-year-olds when Angie, a seven-year-old student from another class, hurried into the room. She stood at my side, shifting from foot to foot as I finished helping Jordan with his print making. "Yes, Angie?"

Figure 5–7   Angie's drawing of a frog: note ears

"Well," she began intently, "you know how our class is studying pond animals? We brought back a frog, and I've been noticing it has these two big circles on his head. Do you know what they are?"

"Big circles, two of them?" I repeated. Angie nodded vigorously. "I think I can help. Did you make a picture of how they look?"

Again she nodded. "Do you want me to get it?"

"I'd love that!" I replied. "That would really help me be sure."

She returned in a moment, breathless. I studied her drawing (Figure 5–7). "Here?" I pointed, "Right behind its eyes?"

She nodded yes. "Do you know what they are?"

"Well, this may seem strange, but those circles are your frog's ears."

Angie looked at her picture, then at me, incredulous.

"They aren't much like your ears, are they?" I asked.

Angie laughed. "No!"

"Well, your ears have this big part on the outside that we can see, and other parts, like the eardrum, inside. But frogs don't have the big outside part. They hear with those two circles you discovered."

Angie was fascinated by what I had told her. She spent most of the afternoon poring over books about frogs, studying the pictures and copying them onto drawing paper (see Figure 5–7). However, as I consider the incident now, I wish I had responded differently. My straightforward answer linked her to me, and to the authors of the various books she consulted, in a limited way. When she had questions, we would answer. She could take note.

What might I have done differently, to make Angie more of a collaborator than a dependent? And how might I have positioned her to proceed when no teacher or book could supply an answer? Further, how might I have implied that she could, and perhaps should, evaluate the information I gave her and consider its credibility?

Often, I do so by helping children design simple investigations that may answer their questions. I didn't take this route with Angie, because I had no idea how she could discover the function of those two big circles for herself. Some research requires understanding, skills, or equipment that is beyond the capacity of elementary school children. Looking back, though, I see that urging firsthand investigation or relaying facts were not my only options. I could have focused on the "story" behind the facts as well as on the facts themselves. In Angie's case, I might have done so by saying, "I've been told that those circles are your frog's ears. Can you believe it? I wonder how anyone figured that out?" The change in phrasing is minor, but I think it shifts the conversation significantly.

To see how, just think of any point about the natural world that you have come to accept, such as cats catch mice or male cardinals are red or ice is less dense than water. Whatever it is, consider why you believe it is true. Then imagine how you would possibly establish or confirm this fact if you had to. I find that even young children are ready to tackle this kind of thinking. When they do, they are more likely to view inquiry as a process of "trying to find out" rather than "looking it up," and they are able to think critically about information they uncover.

Elementary Ethics

An important, but too often neglected, aspect of science teaching involves dealing with values and ethics. Opportunities for this are many. The instructions that come with our incubator tell us that by opening one egg every few days, we can directly observe the dramatic changes in the developing chicken embryo. However, this procedure will kill the embryo as well as allow for observation. What do we want to do? Later, when the chicks hatch, the children will want to hold and cuddle them every minute. How much handling is good for a baby chick? Perhaps less than what is good for children. A spotted salamander is brought to school early one spring. Students are fascinated by this seldom-seen animal and want to keep and study it. However, it has been collected in the middle of its brief breeding season—what should we do?

When questions like this surface (and they always do) I usually have children meet to discuss the options. Sometimes, a group is quick to arrive at an answer that satisfies everyone, but often the class is divided (see Chapter 7, pp. 119–20). Frequently, we simply lack the information necessary to choose a wise course of action. In these cases students may need to consult books, local experts, state or federal laws, their own data, or their own values before setting class policy. I may have research to do as well. All this can be time consuming. However, when we hurry on with our science projects, glossing over concerns or ignoring the consequences of our actions, we say to children that it does not matter what effect our work has on the world around us—scientists pursuing investigations do not need to bother about such things. When we take the time to consider our values and those of others (including those that have been translated into conservation laws or other relevant restrictions) we say to children that it is important to be responsible and considerate, in both our classroom and the world.

Classroom Culture and Science Content

In elementary school classrooms, science content and the context in which children attend to it are not separable. Worthwhile subject matter must be a part of our science program from the beginning. Otherwise, we cannot expect children to invest in working, thinking, and paying attention during meetings. Eleanor Duckworth (1978), in her review of the African Primary Science Program, writes: "I react strongly against the thought that we need to provide children with only a set of intellectual processes—a dry, contentless set of tools that they can go about applying. I believe that the tools cannot help developing once children have something real to think about; and if they don't have anything real to think about, they won't be applying tools anyway" (27).

I strongly agree. I also believe that what we teach and how we teach (or what we learn and how we learn) are connected. Just as children must have worthwhile content to think about in order to invest their energy in learning, they must have a classroom environment in which thinking and working are possible. Children unused to cooperating, collaborating, and considering one another's ideas will need to learn new ways of working together as they go about the business of observing and discovering the phenomena of the world around them. Careful attention at the beginning of the year to "how to be together at meeting" helps ensure a dependable and respectful working climate and leaves teacher and children increasingly able to focus on interesting scientific observations and questions as the year progresses. And a continuing focus on what each classmate, teacher, and professional expert thinks—and why—fosters the kind of classroom culture I strive for. In it, all sincere ideas are appreciatively received and given consideration. At the same time, all are open to question.

Facilitating Meetings: Some Practical Reminders

Make it safe. Avoid burdening children with an unnecessarily elaborate code of conduct, but develop any "meeting manners" that ensure each contribution will be received with interest and respect. Children often know what they need in this regard and can propose guidelines for the class to live by.

Follow a predictable format. A predictable format can free children to focus on new information and ideas, as can efficient transitions to and from the meeting.

Match meeting length to children's ability to attend. Sitting still, listening to others, and contributing ideas in a group can be taxing. While I have seen a group of second-graders stay excited and involved for forty minutes, this is not always possible. Younger children can sometimes manage just ten or fifteen, and even fifth- and sixth-graders can get wiggly and distracted if we exceed their limits. Monitor time and attention so that meetings stay interesting and productive.

Choose a focus. Clarity about the purpose of a meeting can help it be productive, so establish the focus at the outset.

Get all the ideas on the table. Use meetings to solicit a wide range of input on a particular topic or question. Find out what children think and also *why*. Call attention to contradictions and puzzles, but suspend judgment. Examine assumptions.

Tolerate "unfinished business." Many meetings will raise more questions than they settle, so don't feel compelled to push for consensus in your facilitation or to weigh in as the "authority." Rather, facilitate thoughtful consideration of a range of ideas and evidence, and recognize the "tentative and provisional" nature of scientific fact.

Encourage collaborations. Use meetings to make links between the work of one child and that of another. Also link children and texts, and children and experts.

Display your own interest, curiosity, and confusion. Enthusiasm is infectious, and the quality of a teacher's attention to subject matter can encourage students likewise. Meetings are also a place to ask for clarification if you are unsure what a student means, and to share your own puzzling observations and tentative ideas. Children will learn from your example.

6 *Helping Children Pursue Their Questions*

When I tackle a particular science unit or try to teach a specific concept, I deliberately ask students to address certain questions. Sometimes, I even dictate how they must do so. For example, if I want children to understand that soils vary and that their particular properties may make them useful to us and to other organisms in a range of ways, I ask children to collect soil samples from the schoolyard and neighborhood. I also ask them to sort their samples by color and texture and subject them to a range of tests. I make no apology for this. Catastrophes ranging from the Dust Bowl to the pollution of coastal waters by septic system leach fields convince me we'd all be better off if we knew more about soil. Children may not, on their own, be aware that they can learn important things by sifting soil through a series of coarse and fine sieves or by shaking it in a tube of water. In fact, they might not even think soil is worthy of their attention. I try to make clear that it is.

I also try to share my role as curriculum planner with my students and make sure that their interests and questions also shape our science studies. I'd find it difficult to nurture their curiosity and ability to investigate otherwise. However, sharing this role complicates my work. I am best equipped to help children pursue paths that I myself have explored, and when I share the reins, children seldom stick to these paths.

When we give up teaching from established lesson plans or scripted programs, we relinquish the comfort of having stock answers for stock questions. We give our attention to children as they work, supporting their efforts and enabling them to move ahead with new ideas and projects. Children, free to pursue their own questions, head off in various directions. The situations that result may be familiar and expected, or they may take us by surprise. Learning what children are intrigued or puzzled by and figuring out what might be helpful in each unique situation is the work we take on. Essentially, we become children's research advisors as they plan and launch investigations of varying size and sophistication. Our guidance can foster their capacity to solve problems and to generate more.

Suggest Another Look

There are times when a direct question deserves a direct answer. However, this usually isn't my first response when teaching science. Many of the questions children raise are ones they can answer themselves, and it serves my broad aims if I can position children to do so rather than tell them what I think. Sometimes, if I simply have children review what they already know, they are able to put their ideas together in a new way that sheds light on a puzzle. Other times, they themselves can gather the information they've requested by extending their initial observations.

That was simple to arrange for five-year-old Joshua, who was looking rather uneasily at the class guinea pig as he considered whether to pat it.

Josh: Does he have teeth?

Ellen D.: You can check and see. I'll hold him up so you can see his mouth better.

Josh: He does! Long teeth.

Ellen D.: He uses those teeth to eat. But if you're worried that he might bite you instead of his food, I'll hold him like this—facing me—and you can touch him here on his back.

On another occasion, Janet, age seven, was wondering about crickets. "How do they chirp?" she asked.

"Let's watch your cricket for a few minutes," I suggested. "Maybe we'll be able to tell."

We watched. Eventually the cricket chirped again.

"I saw it!" Janet exclaimed. "When it chirped, it kind of chattered its wings."

In both of these instances children raised questions to which their own observations readily provided answers.

Not all questions can be addressed by simply taking another look, but those that can be should be given over to children to answer. I don't like to tease children by withholding information they have requested, but I do want them to investigate their surroundings directly and become competent problem solvers. Children's own activity can effectively further those aims. However, along with the suggestion to "see for yourself," it's important to offer support so that children feel encouraged to take action rather than daunted by the prospect. In the previous example, Josh and Janet needed minimal support. Happily, that is often the case.

Monitor Events

Another opportunity to encourage children to answer their own questions occurred one morning when a class of eight- and nine-year-olds arrived to discover a hole chipped in one of the chicken eggs they'd been incubating and saw a small beak pushing at the shell. Although they remained on watch for half an hour, the chick widened its hole only slightly in that time.

"How long does it take them to hatch?" Erin wondered, giving voice to a question that was probably on several minds.

"This chick doesn't seem to be getting out very fast, does it?" I acknowledged. "Is there a way you could find out how long it takes?"

Erin considered. "Well, we could just keep on watching it. We could write down what the time was when we noticed it was hatching and the time when it's hatched."

"Then we could figure out how much time had gone by," chimed in Carla.

Aware that this event was proceeding slowly and also of the reading and math work I had planned, I anticipated interruptions in the children's vigil. "What if you need to take a break from watching to go do something else for a while?" I asked.

"We could keep coming back to check," Adam proposed. "Like at the end of each period, or every ten minutes or something."

"That sounds like a plan that will work."

Indeed it was, and the children were able to supply themselves with a partial answer to their question by timing how long this particular chick took to get out of its shell. (One of the children captured the process in the series of drawings shown in Figure 6–1.)

Figure 6–1   Drawing of a chick hatching by boy, age eight

Days later the children retrieved a book about chickens from the classroom library and read this:

> After three weeks' incubation, the chick is ready to emerge. It jabs at the underside of the shell with a special egg tooth on its beak, working its way around the middle of the egg. This process is known as "pipping" and can take anywhere from twenty minutes to fourteen hours to complete. (Oxford Scientific Films 1979, 3)

This information was an exciting find, as it both confirmed and extended the children's firsthand research. It was as if they were reviewing their own data alongside a paper published by a distant colleague and finding that it fit within the established range (a range far wider than they had suspected). I could have referred them to the book when Erin first asked how long chicks take to hatch, but that wouldn't have promoted investigation quite as well. I might also have read the passage aloud as the hatching date drew near. While that would have been fine to do, I think the text had greater meaning for the children coming, as it did, on the heels of their direct experience.

Many investigations can be based on children's systematic observations. Children can also incorporate other information. Teach children how to gather scientific information from books, experts, and other sources, and also how to evaluate, interpret, and use what they find (see Teaching Standard D, NRC 1996, 45).

Focus on What Children Know

Teachers can encourage children to use their senses to gather information and also to use the information they have gathered. One fall I took a class hiking along a shallow stream. The children spread out to explore. Some discovered tiny creatures in the water, while others pointed out special rocks or brightly colored mushrooms.

Holly bent down to inspect something. I joined a group of children assembling around her as she knelt beside the brown, dry, spore-bearing stalk of a sensitive fern (see Holly's drawing in Figure 6–2).

HOLLY: What's *that* thing?

DARCY: I think it's dead.

Figure 6–2   **Drawing of a sensitive fern stalk, by girl age eight**

BENNIE: Is it a plant?

JESS: I think I've seen one of those before, but I don't know what they are.

ELLEN D.: Let's see what you've found.

HOLLY: This thing.

ELLEN D.: That's interesting. Do you want to bring it back to school so you can look at it more and try to find out what it is?

HOLLY: Well, yes, but what if it's rare? I know some flowers are rare and you're not supposed to pick them.

ELLEN D.: That's a good point. We shouldn't pick it if it's rare. Is there a way you can find out if it's rare here?

HOLLY: Well, we could look around and see if there are any more.

ELLEN D.: Okay. Let me know what you find.

The children fanned out and searched. They found several groups of the strange brown things—dozens of stalks in all.

ELLEN D.: So you found quite a few?

BENNIE: Thirty, maybe more.

DARCY (*laughing*): I don't think they're too rare, at least not here!

ELLEN D.: What does that make you think, Holly?

HOLLY: That I could pick one or two to bring back.

ELLEN D.: But if you hadn't found very many?

HOLLY: Then it might be rare and we shouldn't pick any.

My idea here was to help the children retrieve and use what they already knew (the meaning of *rare*, the prohibition against picking rare plants) to solve Holly's problem: she wanted to pick a stalk but didn't know if she should. The matter could have been settled more quickly if I had said, "I don't think this is rare. Go ahead and pick it." One advantage of not doing so and instead allowing the group to determine whether the stalk was too rare to pick is that the children might later be able to use this experience to deal with a similar problem. If the solution depended on my particular knowledge or permission, it would not be transferable.

Of course, sometimes it is important to establish and enforce rules rather than leave protocol in the hands of children. For instance, you may know that a particular flower is a threatened species or be responsible for enforcing a botanical garden's "no picking" rule. You may need to dissuade a determined child from bringing home a baby bird. The situation above didn't have such constraints, but by all means set limits if they are needed.

When children bring me questions, I often keep many of my own thoughts about the matter to myself. Instead, I use questions to help children focus on what they know and how they might learn more. This isn't meant to be oblique or annoying. Rather, it is an effort to help children build a repertoire of strategies that they can use when confronted with questions. I want them to feel curious and able to plan their next step— not overwhelmed or frustrated—when there is something they need to know. The questions I pose become a template children can use to think through similar situations.

I have warned against withholding answers to children's questions in a teasing manner. Pretending not to know something that one in fact knows is apt to confuse. We need not worry about having enough opportunity to encourage children to find their own answers, for no matter how great our knowledge, children walking in the woods or working at the science table are sure to uncover something that is mysterious to us, too. Quite often, children are so absorbed with their own questions and puzzles that they do not even look to us for information. I did not worry about whether to tell Holly that the name of her brown stalk was *sensitive fern*, because her *what is it?* was more an exclamation of discovery than a request for a label. She did not repeat the question, and even if she had and I had responded with a name, her mystery would hardly have been solved. That dry brown thing looked nothing like a fern—it didn't even seem alive. When we hand children's questions back to them to answer and they intently go off to "have another look" or breathlessly return to share their latest findings, we have been helpful. If they seem confused, frustrated, or impatient with us, then perhaps the situation calls for another response. Teacher Carolyn Pratt (1948) wrote:

The over-helpful adult is no help, is actually a hindrance to the child. What perceptive adult has not seen a child's face go blank like a closed door at the very moment when he is receiving the most helpful attention? Who has not had the humiliating experience of having a child walk idly away in the middle of an answer to his question?

She continues:

Questions came in a steady stream from some of my children when we first began to go on our trips. But when they got their questions turned back to them—"Why do you think the ferry has two round ends?"— they were silenced for a while. When the questions came again they were different. They were not asked just to get attention, to make conversation, or for the dozen reasons besides that of gaining information. They were sincere and purposeful; the question now became what it should be, the first step in the child's own effort to find the answer for himself. (44–45)

Provide Time and Tools

Nina was quite taken with our stereomicroscope. It was a tool new to her, and she was excited by the world it revealed. Once I showed her how to adjust the focus, she parked herself in front of it. Since we were studying birds at the time, I had put a collection of feathers out for the children to explore. Nina chose to observe a beautiful green parrot feather with red and yellow markings.[1] I wasn't surprised that it caught her attention, or that her microscopic examination of it kept her occupied for a full half-hour. But I was surprised when she plunked herself down at the microscope again the next day and continued to study the very same feather! I was curious and inquired about her work.

Nina explained that she had discovered something about the green color of the feather. When she looked at it without the microscope, parts of the feather looked solid green. But under magnification, she could see that wasn't true. The feather actually had only a tiny bit of green, located in particular places. The rest of the area appeared black. I looked through the microscope and saw the feather exactly as she had described it. I

1. Before collecting feathers for classroom use, familiarize yourself with state and federal restrictions. You must obtain a special permit to possess feathers, nests, or other remains from migratory birds and birds of prey. Alternatively, you may be able to borrow specimens from a local nature center or museum. Pet stores, farmers, hunters, craft stores, and suppliers of fly-tying material are also potential sources.

encouraged her to draw what she had seen and to check out the red and yellow markings on the feather as well.

Nina continued her examination of the parrot feather for nearly two weeks. Her excitement grew as she observed the various ways the different colors in the feather were configured. She discovered that not only did colors appear different microscopically, they "behaved" differently, too. Some colors stayed the same when the feather was tilted or held to the light, while others changed or "disappeared"! My excitement grew along with Nina's. I listened to her daily updates, occasionally supplying a term or asking a question to help her clarify her thoughts. Mostly, though, I just let her continue.

Feather colors can be due to pigments, the interplay of light and the structure of the feather, or both. Nina's interest in the microscope led her to this fascinating borderland of ornithology and optics, one that professional scientists continue to investigate.

The *Standards* remind us that it takes time to develop scientific understanding. Teachers must therefore find time for students to carry out extended investigations. Access to science tools and materials is crucial as well (NRC 1996, 44, 218). Nina's study of feathers was inspired by, and depended on, the microscope.

Encourage Experiments

Sometimes children can devise simple experiments to learn about things that puzzle them. This was my solution for a small group of eight-year-olds who were forcing tulip bulbs. They had carefully observed and drawn the bulbs they had selected, then planted them in clay pots filled with soil. The pots were put in an unheated part of the school building for two cold weeks in February, then brought into the classroom and watered.

After just a few days of warmth and water the children noticed tiny green sprouts in the pots. "Our tulips are growing!" they announced with excitement. Over the next few days, more green sprouts appeared, more by far than the number of bulbs that had been planted. The children watched as tiny, paired leaves developed on each sprout.

"These don't look that much like tulips," Ginger said skeptically.

"They look like weeds!" remarked Nathan.

"You're right! They do look like weeds," Charlene nodded, and the children came over to report their new idea to me.

"So you think these things that are growing in your pots aren't tulips after all, but are something else?" I inquired.

"Yes, aren't they?"

"Well, what have you observed that makes you think so?"

"They look just like weeds," Nathan explained.

"And besides, there's too many of them. I have four growing in my pot but I only planted two tulip bulbs," continued Patrick.

"And they aren't growing in the right places, either," Charlene added.

I considered this information. "I can see why you think they might be weeds instead of tulips," I said. "Can you think of a way to find out for sure?" I wanted the children to use evidence rather than the weight of my opinion to settle the matter.

A few ideas were proposed: digging up the tiny sprouts to see whether they were growing out of the tulip bulbs, comparing the sprouts to some other weeds, and so on. In the end, the children decided that the simplest solution would be to continue with their daily observations and see if anything else grew in the pots. They stapled blank paper to make journals in which they could log what happened and kept careful track. Nearly two weeks after the first green sprouts appeared, the children discovered new, larger sprouts pushing out of the soil. These looked more like tulips, they all agreed. Discussing the situation, I returned to a question that had been brought up earlier by one of the children but had been forgotten. "How did those weeds end up growing in your flower pots? Did you plant them?"

Of course they had not; they had planted only tulip bulbs. But they did have some ideas about how such a thing could have happened.

"Maybe some weed seeds were in the dirt to begin with. Then when we watered the dirt they just started growing," Nathan suggested.

"Or maybe some seeds blew in from somewhere else," Ginger proposed.

I might have supported these explanations, then let the whole thing go, but again I pushed for confirmation. "How could you find out if your hypotheses are correct? Both ideas sound like possible explanations for what happened. Is there a way to be more sure?"

"You'd have to do an experiment," Ginger said.

"What sort of experiment might work?" I asked. There were no responses. "Well, let's look at this first hypothesis. Nathan thought that maybe there were some weed seeds in the dirt to begin with. How could you tell if there were?"

"You could look at the dirt," Ricky suggested. "You could put some under the microscope and see if you see any seeds."

"That sounds like a big job," I said, "but worth a try."

"Or we could just look around in the dirt," Nathan offered. "Maybe we would find some seeds."

"We could borrow a sifter from another class," said Patrick, "They have sifters in the sand table. Remember? We used to use them."

"You have a few ideas to work on to try to see if the hypothesis about weed seeds being in the potting soil might be true. Is there any thing else you want to try?"

"I have an idea!" said Charlene. "We could fill a pot up with dirt, but not plant anything in the dirt. Then we could water it and see if anything grows."

Here are two reports on the ensuing work, in the children's own words:

> We had a hypothesis that there was a seed in the soil that we were using for our tulips. Me and Patrick got a sifter and started sifting through the dirt. Lo and behold we found a little weed that was attached to a seed. Our hypothesis was right. (Ricky, age eight)

> We planted soil to see if anything was in the soil because little green plants were growing in our tulip pots that we didn't plant, we wanted to know what they were. The results were: nothing grew. The reason we think is there wasn't any seed in the part of the soil we planted but there were in other parts. (Ginger, age eight, and Charlene, age seven)

Gathering and interpreting evidence is at the heart of the scientific enterprise. When children propose explanations, urge them to put their explanations to the test and seek evidence to support their claims. Construct a classroom schedule that makes this possible (see Teaching Standard D, NRC 1996, 43–44).

Ginger's journal drawings of the progression of her observations is shown in Figure 6–3.

Appreciate Meandering Inquiries, Redirect Unproductive Ones

The tulip growers above enjoyed using impressive, scientific-sounding words like *experiment* and *hypothesis* to describe their work, and I enjoy introducing children to such terms. However, I know the situations in

A: Tulip bulbs before being planted

1.

2.

B: Weeds start growing

There's some kind of groth!

I Think it might be a weed but maybe not!

C: Third petal starts growing

It still has That Groth But it's growing a 3rd pedate

Finaly my tulip's growing! yea!

Figure 6–3 Tulip Journal by Ginger, age eight

(continued)

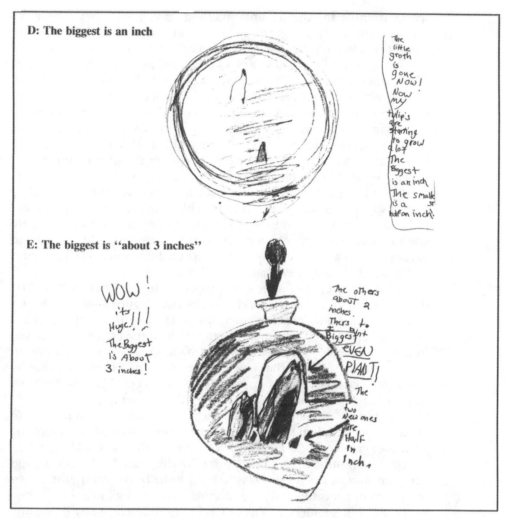

Figure 6–3   Continued

which children are apt to apply them may lack some qualities that professional scientists require. Ricky, age eight, considered the presence of
a single seedling adequate proof of his hypothesis, and Nathan felt that
"looking around in the dirt" was as specific as he needed to be about
his experimental procedure. It is important to help children develop
an increasingly sophisticated understanding of scientific inquiry over
the course of their elementary school years. Along the way, we need to
appreciate that children's investigations may not be as linear as our own

school training in "the scientific method" may imply they should be. Children are, after all, beginning to learn how to pose questions of nature and get answers. It is our job to encourage them to articulate investigable questions, control variables, weigh evidence, and consider any number of other things (see Teaching Standards B and E, NRC 1996, 32–37, 43–51). We can also appreciate the value in work that is more meandering or less well defined, and gently redirect if it becomes unproductive.

Dylan's cricket studies are a case in point. Dylan and three of his second-grade classmates examined a cage full of crickets over the course of several weeks. I offered little direction to shape their work, wondering, instead, what the children would find interesting or of value.

Dylan and his partner Tommy made a special pet of one cricket they named Zipper. Dylan spent hours watching Zipper. As he did, he exclaimed over what he noticed—to me, to his group, and to himself. He was careful never to touch Zipper, in case the cricket might bite. (Dylan explained that a shiny cricket in his backyard had once bit him, and it had hurt.) He also noticed that the cricket cage stank.

Dylan considered what he knew about the sounds crickets make and drew a picture of a cricket "making tunes" (see Figure 6–4). "We hear a lot of peeps down there at my basement, so I'm sure they sing like that," he explained. He also said that his family killed the crickets they found in their basement, partly because they made so much noise but also in case they were the kind that bite. He shared many other things that he knew about crickets. For instance, he was sure that crickets hatched from eggs, because he had seen cricket eggs in his basement.

Dylan was fascinated with his crickets' movements and decided to observe and record all the different things Zipper did. At one point, he let Zipper crawl around on a piece of paper so that he could get a better view. Naturally, Zipper ran off, but Tommy caught the cricket and corralled him under a clear-plastic petri dish. Dylan continued to observe him in his confinement, muttering, "He's going in circles . . . he's starting . . . he's going . . . Zipper's going in different ways. He's going different ways." As he talked, he drew a line around the outside of the petri dish that imitated the circular path of the cricket, explaining as he went along: "I'm not drawing, I'm making cir—it's going in circles. So this is how—I'm figuring out. Why is he going in circles?" He added arrows to indicate the direction in which Zipper traveled. Eventually, he came to call this his "study picture." He seemed to regard the circular movements as a distinct form of cricket behavior, unrelated to the petri dish.

Dylan returned Zipper to the petri dish the following week and made another study picture to document the cricket's behavior. He used arrows to show that Zipper had jumped up and down. He then drew a spi-

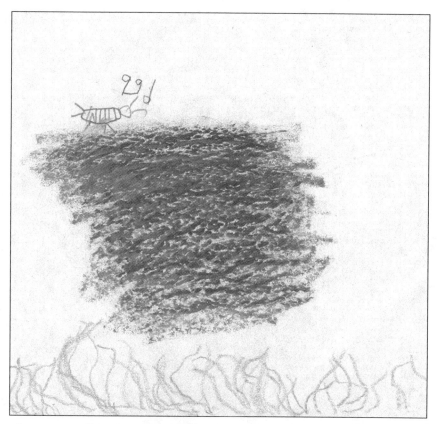

Figure 6–4 Dylan's picture of a cricket "making tunes"

ral path on a piece of paper (see Figure 6–5) and placed the petri dish on top. He wanted to see if Zipper would follow the path. (Zipper didn't). He also made mazes for his cricket to follow. (The outcome was similar.)

Dylan looked at a book about crickets that one of the children had brought in but soon stated, "I'm not learning anything from this." Apparently, it did not address his particular interest in what crickets do.

At one point, Dylan became quite frustrated. "I'm not getting much studying," he complained, "I think I might as well draw a picture." The problem, I learned, was that he wanted to see Zipper do "all sorts of different things, but he's not doing anything." I was surprised to hear this, for it looked like Zipper was circling around in his petri dish. This did not seem significant to Dylan, though, for he had seen this behavior already. It brought him some satisfaction to list, over the course of several sessions, each new observation he made (see Figure 6–6). I encouraged

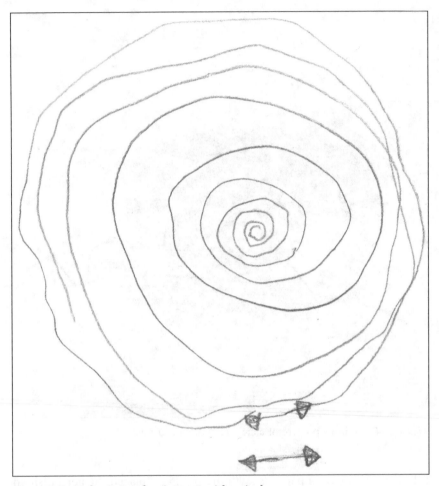

Figure 6–5   Dylan's "study picture" with spiral

him to do so, but I also tried to help him accept the fact that the rate at
which scientific study yielded new discoveries could sometimes be slow.
During the lulls, I suggested additional lines of inquiry, such as learning
how his cricket apportioned its time, interacted with others, or made use
of its environment.

Dylan's work focused on the characteristics and behavior of crickets
(see Content Standard C, NRC 1996, 127–29). Learning to articulate
questions that can be investigated is a new challenge for him.

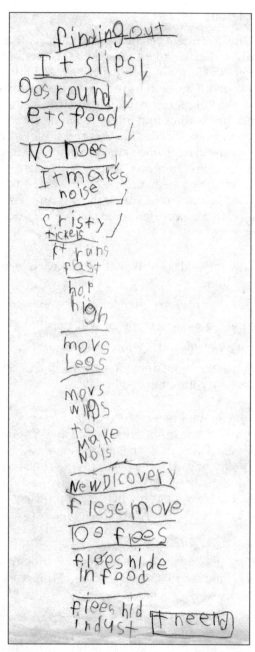

Figure 6–6   **Dylan's list of discoveries**

Help Define a Focus

Sometimes children are interested in a topic and eager to get to work, but they flounder when they try to establish the specifics of their research. Perhaps their topic is so broad or their experience so limited that they are unable to come up with a question they are able to investigate. Or the topic might lend itself to more abstract or sophisticated work than they can manage, and they cannot find a way to approach it that is concrete enough for them to understand. This was the situation with Brad and Jason, two nine-year-old boys who came to school one day excited about the events of the previous afternoon. During a play date, they had mixed baking soda and vinegar together. Now they wanted to repeat the experiment so the whole class could watch the mixture fizz. While searching for a container, they discovered some plastic tubes with stoppers and rushed over to me.

BRAD: Look what we found! Is it okay if we put the vinegar and baking soda in one of these?

ELLEN D.: What do you think will happen?

BRAD: Well, the baking soda and vinegar will start to fizz.

JASON (*with an impish grin*): And the top will blow off!

ELLEN D.: And you'd like to see that happen! Well, let's see if we can figure out a way to try it that would be safe.

The boys came up with two solutions. The first was to cork the filled tube and leave it on its side in the sink so that any "explosion" would be contained. The second was to hold the tube champagne-bottle style so the cork would fly up toward some overhanging cupboards (rather than toward lights, windows, or faces). They chose the second and were delighted when the top blew off as predicted. (In retrospect, waiting to try the experiment until we had purchased safety glasses would have been wise.)

During the following week Brad and Jason repeated their "experiment" many times (mostly on the playground during recess). However, after a few days I could see that the repetition of this work was not holding their interest. I suggested a meeting.

ELLEN D.: You were right that baking soda and vinegar fizz when they're mixed together, and you've shown how that reaction can pop the cork out of a test tube. What would you like to try next?

BRAD: Well, we don't really know.

ELLEN D.: Is this something you want to keep working on, or do you want to switch to another project?

JASON: We like this! We're just not sure what to do next.

Moments like this underscore the value of having some familiarity with the subject matter. When children are out of ideas, it helps to hear some new options. My experience with fizzing chemicals is not extensive, but I thought perhaps it would be fruitful to have the boys consider the properties of a few additional chemicals and discover how they react with one another. I forged ahead.

ELLEN D.: Here are a few possibilities. You can think them over and let me know if you want to try one. One thing you might want to do is to try to find out if any other chemicals react like baking soda and vinegar. We'd have to figure out how to do it safely. Some chemicals just fizz when you mix them together, but others can be really dangerous!

BRAD: We already found out one other thing that fizzes: baking powder and vinegar.

ELLEN D.: So you've made a start.

JASON: Alka-Seltzer fizzes, too. That's how we got started.

BRAD: Isn't it because there's an acid and a base or something in it?

ELLEN D.: Acids and bases are two important groups of chemicals. Another project you could do is to find out more about acids and bases: what they are, what they can do. Still another possibility is to try to get this reaction you know about to do some work for you. Once I saw a really neat machine. It was a waterwheel that was powered when the gas from fizzing baking soda and vinegar pushed some water out of a container and onto a waterwheel. Maybe you could invent a machine that is driven by vinegar and baking soda power, or a vehicle that can move.

The next day, they returned with a project in mind.

JASON: We're going to make a rocket.

ELLEN D.: Neat! Do you have an idea about how you'll build it?

JASON: Well, kind of. We'll use one of these tubes. But we don't know what else.

ELLEN D.: Look around on the project shelves and see what you can find. When you have an idea of how you want to go about it, sketch out a plan and bring it to me.

BRAD: What do you mean, a plan?

ELLEN D.: Remember when we made birdfeeders? Kids drew a picture of how the finished birdfeeder would look and listed the materials and steps they thought they would follow. Your rocket might not turn out exactly like your plan, but I do want to see some kind of a plan. (The plan they devised is shown in Figure 6–7.)

After a few days of construction with plastic tubes, Styrofoam meat trays, masking tape, and marker caps, the boys were ready to try their rocket. I watched from the window. There were a few false starts that left the ground crew muttering and shaking vinegar off their hands before they succeeded in getting the rocket to lift off. It reached a height of a foot or two before it splashed down on the playground. They returned to the room excited and full of ideas about how to improve their rocket's performance.

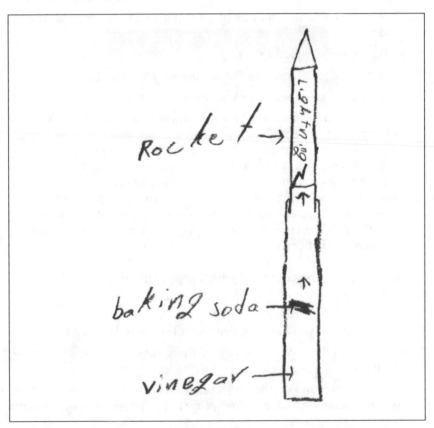

Figure 6–7   Jason's plan for a baking soda-and-vinegar-powered rocket

"The baking soda and vinegar mix too fast," Jason complained. "They start fizzing before we can get the top on, then it doesn't go very high."

Brad identified the next research priority. "We have to keep them separate."

Over the next week or so, they devised a way to separate the baking soda and vinegar with a thin layer of tissue that would eventually dissolve and allow a delayed blast off. Another child joined the team, and the rocket was rebuilt several times. The second generation of rockets popped up to a height of four to six feet. The boys again approached me. "Now we want to try a car!"

I watched for a few days and noticed work on the car was not proceeding in a very directed way. I suggested another meeting.

JASON: We don't really want to do the car idea. It's pretty much the same as a rocket—it just goes sideways instead of up.

ELLEN D.: What about another kind of research?

BRAD: Yeah, like that acids and bases idea.

ELLEN D.: What do you know about acids and bases?

Not surprisingly, their ideas about acids and bases were vague. But their interest was strong, and they began a new project (testing for acids and bases) with enthusiasm. They were exposed to the notion of pH, and determined that a number of familiar household substances could be placed with vinegar in the "acids" category. When children have a broad or ill-defined interest, or are curious about a complicated topic, they can investigate some aspect of it if helped to narrow their focus and to select an appropriate starting place.

Children's Particular Observations and Scientific Generalizations

I once visited a science class in which the teacher had provided his pupils with live beetles and some time to look at them. The children seemed quite interested: they were just bursting with reactions and observations.

"Ooh—look at mine!"

"Gross—I'm not touching that!"

"Hey—they are fast!"

"I've got two brown ones and a black one."

"This one's dead."

It was a lively beginning. But then, to my surprise, the teacher quickly collected the dead beetles and discarded them, saying, in effect, nothing important can be learned from these! Next, he began questioning the class about what they had noticed.

"How many body parts did you see?"

"Four," a girl offered.

The teacher asked her to explain.

"Well, there's a head, and a body, and a wing on each side," she replied.

Now, if your high school biology class covered the same ground mine did, you know that "four" is the wrong answer. The teacher quickly sketched a beetle on the chalkboard and proceeded to explain: there were not, in fact, four body parts on these beetles—insects had but three. Each had a head, a thorax, and an abdomen. The girl looked puzzled. After all, her beetle had two wings, right there on its back! A few other children also seemed confused: how could it be that legs were not a body part? What sense did that make?

It isn't hard to see what motivated this teacher's approach. He was attempting to introduce his class to some general characteristics that scientists have determined insects share. These characteristics, which include six jointed legs and an exoskeleton with three major body parts, distinguish insects from other kinds of animals. Surely that is worth knowing. The children simply weren't ready to know it yet. They were meeting mealworm beetles for the first time, and the girl who had been called on had no reason to think that the teacher's "three parts" were the only ones to focus on. Nor did her beetle represent insects in general. It was a specific, particular creature to her. The lessons it had to offer were about its own self, not about the taxonomic class to which it had been assigned. The generalization that all insects have three body parts and a hard exoskeleton, rigidly applied, has convinced more than one child that caterpillars are not insects.

Much school science work is anchored in generalizations or abstract principles that integrate the findings of many different people who have focused on specific but related situations over the course of years. When we want to acquaint children with these facts, we sometimes choose specific situations, creatures, or demonstrations that we believe will illustrate them for students and show that they are true. The trouble arises when students who have not yet done much "groundwork" in a particular area remain focused on specifics. The girl above wasn't thinking about insects in general or taxonomic distinctions between insects and other classes of arthropods. She was thinking about her beetle. Each one of its parts was of equal importance.

I once worked with a second-grade class who also focused on small animals. Their subjects included spiders, giant cockroaches, silkworms, and monarch caterpillars. The overarching concept I was required to get across was that animals have life cycles. To some extent, children attended to this agenda. They marveled as each caterpillar transformed itself into a chrysalis and then emerged as a butterfly. They were fascinated when the spiders produced egg cases and wanted to see the babies emerge. But I was struck by the degree to which each unfolding life remained distinct for the children. It was the individual organisms and the details of their existence that fascinated, not the common theme of a life cycle.

Nor were children much interested in some of the distinctions that adults commonly make. I looked on during a field trip to a local university as several graduate students in entomology conversed with the children. The children had brought cages containing animals they'd been studying and the graduate students had prepared a wonderful and informative program, illustrated with slides and specimens. Each group had to stretch to understand the other's focus. For example, the entomologists assumed that the "insect" category was important and also easy to understand (exoskeleton, six legs, three body parts, and all that). The children found it irrelevant and also unclear. They especially had questions about caterpillars how fit in, as the ones they were intimate with lacked distinct body parts and seemed to have more than six legs. The children also had questions about their giant cockroaches, but mostly, I think, they just wanted to share them with an appreciative audience. Several children, who typically kept one on or near them as they did their morning work, could distinguish between the different individuals, both in terms of appearance and "personality." The scientists seemed both impressed and amused at this level of knowledge. They also studied giant cockroaches, but were not on such intimate terms.

Second-graders are perhaps especially focused on particulars, but it is worth remembering that any individual's ability to classify and generalize develops over time when trying to teach concepts that demand these skills.

Plants and animals have life cycles, and children's science studies can acquaint them with the particulars of some of these (Content Standard C, NRC 1996, 129). Direct contact with actual organisms will yield a wealth of other information as well.

Helping Children Do Research

It is exciting for children to seek answers to their own important questions. Elementary school children often need help framing questions and carrying out research projects. Here are some ways that teachers can assist:

Listen for questions as children observe and explore. What puzzles or intrigues particular students?

Keep track of children's questions. Journals, science notebooks, tape recorders, or a chart posted on the wall can serve the purpose.

Bring children back to their questions. "Remember yesterday, when you were wondering what kind of bird this feather came from? How could you find out?"

Call attention to puzzles or inconsistencies that have come up. "John says the pan of ice on the windowsill is nearly melted, while the one in the coat closet is not. What do you make of that?"

Discuss various ways a particular question or problem could be approached. Some children will base their ideas on problems they have previously tackled or on things they have heard about the work of adult scientists. Encourage them to explain the connection between the other research they know about and the problem at hand.

Discuss the merits and difficulties associated with each research possibility, then ask children which approach they'd like to try first. Be ready to help them follow any safe and reasonable plan, whether or not it is your favorite.

Help children map out a basic research strategy and consider important details. Your questions and occasional directions can enable them to break down big jobs into small, manageable steps. "What kind of person would know about birds? How can you find her phone number? What do you want to ask her?"

Encourage children to discuss ethical and practical issues as they arise. "Since you want to find out what is inside this rock but it doesn't belong to you, what can you do?" "What might you do with these crickets now that you have finished your study?" "Where will you set up your experiment? When can you work on it?"

Rehearse new strategies and techniques with children. "Before you try using this mirror to look in the real bird's nest, see if you can use it to spot the eggs in this fake nest." "I'll pretend I'm the vet. You call me up and ask your question." "Did anyone ever use a magnifying glass? How did you hold it?"

Plan class meetings and small-group discussions that allow researchers to consult with classmates and share work in progress.
Monitor the level of interest and frustration children experience. Also note the amount of help or direction they seem to need. Be ready to discuss problems and modify plans.

Children's research will answer some questions but prompt many others. Some children find this thrilling, others get frustrated. Help those who crave a more conclusive enterprise to develop a more positive or realistic perspective. Pointing out what children have learned or accomplished—even though they might not have settled a particular question—sometimes helps.

7 *Drawing as Inquiry*

Eight-year-old Adrian sits at a table, drawing a twig retrieved from a jar of water on the windowsill. The twig looks quite different from when Adrian collected it three weeks ago. He described these changes at the beginning of the work period, explaining that the bark had turned from red to green, that the twig had "started budding," and that leaves had come out of the buds. Two leaves had emerged from some of the buds, and Adrian counted even more (up to ten!) from others. He also noticed one unopened bud near the base of his twig. Now, he works with concentration, rarely distracted by a nearby group of children who are happily (and noisily) sewing costumes for a play. He frequently looks up from his drawing to observe his twig. Pairs and clusters of leaves are already penciled along the branches he has drawn; after comparing picture and twig, Adrian adds a few more. He chats with a friend across the table as he puts the final touches on his outline. Another child exclaims over a specimen under the microscope, and Adrian gets up for a look. He returns to add color to his outline, making the leaves a bright green and the bark a darker green. Finally, he colors the very bottom of the main stem brown, then adds a touch of red because "there's both red and brown" on the actual twig. (Adrian's drawing is shown in Figure 7–1.)

Beautiful, carefully executed drawings like Adrian's are commonplace in classrooms where drawing is central to science work. Other kinds of drawings materialize as well: quickly sketched plans, theories, and emerging ideas; pictured procedures, predictions, and results. The process that yields these "science drawings" is sometimes carried out quickly, but often it is time-consuming. And while it seems second nature to some children, it can be challenging—even frustrating—for others. Nonetheless, I encourage (and sometimes require) children to draw.

I merge drawing with elementary science because I believe that drawing can be a powerful way to learn about the world. Drawing enables us to record observations, discover relationships, work out ideas,

Figure 7–1 **Drawing of a twig by Adrian, age eight**

and share information with others. It is simultaneously a form of expression and a mode of inquiry, for whenever we attempt to capture aspects of what we see and understand on paper, the process pushes us to further observation and thought.

It is not unusual for teachers to view writing in this light. Nancie Atwell (1990, xiii) reminds us that writing is basic to thinking and learning in every subject because it is a way to identify problems and solve them and also a way to discover meaning. Furman (2007) elaborates, noting that as we put words on paper, we begin to remember things we have forgotten and relate ideas to one another in new ways. We realize what we know and also what we don't know or are uncertain of. As we write, we are forced to compare and contrast ideas, consider connections, and develop new ways of perceiving our subject. "In a very real sense," Furman explains, "we write our way into a new relationship with the topic" (2). Teachers who share this point of view ask children to write throughout the school day. Their students write to explore mathematical strategies, respond to literature, and analyze social situations.

It is uncommon for drawing to be so well and broadly utilized. I like to be in classrooms where pencils, crayons, and other drawing materials are always within easy reach and where children *do* reach for them—spontaneously and often—with gestures that mean "let me show you" and "let me think." In these classrooms, teachers make room for doodling and decorating, but they realize that drawing has far more to offer. It is a true "language for learning," one that can deepen a child's relationship with many topics if we structure schoolwork to tap its potential.[1] Drawing in various forms can serve children as they investigate their surroundings, and teachers need to create a climate for science study in which all children (not just "the artists") draw to describe and discover.

Attending to the Object: "It Helps You Notice"

A lot of my energy as a science teacher is spent helping children pay attention to some aspect of the world around them. All scientific inquiry begins with such attention, so I encourage children to be observant and to think about what they see. Encouraging them to draw sometimes amounts to the same thing.

When children observe objects or living things and decide (or are told) to draw what they notice, many strive to make what they put on paper "match" the real thing. In an effort to show what it looks like, children shift their attention from paper to object and back again. Even when they have already established considerable familiarity with their subject, drawing it can push children to gather additional information. As one sixth-grader explained, "It helps you notice the details. . . . I keep looking at the rock, then I draw, then I look. . . . It just helps you notice more."

Children's initial observations are often wide-ranging, and when they sit down to draw, they have a good general idea of what they want to show. However, specific questions soon surface. The caterpillar is striped, but is the pattern yellow, black, then white, or are the colors in a different order? It has legs, but how many? In order to create a likeness children require answers, so they take another, more focused, look.

Adrian, above, is a case in point. Before ever setting pencil to paper, he observed and described his twig. But as he attempted to draw it, his desire to produce an accurate representation made him take another look and yet another. Details that had initially escaped his attention or

---

1. The title of Cohen and Gainer's book *Art: Another Language for Learning* (1995) captures the way I view drawing. The text offers an inspiring and accessible discussion of children, art, and education. For other valuable perspectives, see Gallus (1994), Seefeldt (2005), Project Zero and Reggio Children (2001), Edwards, Gandini, and Forman (1993), and Smith et al. (1998).

slipped from memory were considered. His finished "picture" is the product of an extended interaction with the twig that increased his familiarity with it.

Part of the value of drawing in elementary science is simply that it takes time. It keeps children in the company of an object long enough for them to become familiar with it. Certainly, there are children who need no such device. However, there have been many occasions in my teaching experience when a child tried to "move on" after only a passing glance. Sustained, close attention to the material world and extended interaction with it are fundamental to scientific inquiry. And while drawing isn't the only way to encourage these things, it is a perfectly good way, and one many children enjoy.

What Is Known, Unknown, and Uncertain

As they draw their way into a new relationship with their subject, children begin to realize what they know and what they don't know. New discoveries can follow. Eight-year-olds Marcy and Tianna experienced this when they spent a loud and lively afternoon exclaiming over a cage of crickets. Everything the little creatures did amazed, alarmed, or disgusted the girls, and over the course of forty minutes they amassed a wealth of information about how the insects moved, ate, and interacted with one another.

Though record keeping was not their main purpose, the girls drew pictures off and on, sometimes in response to my suggestion and sometimes of their own accord. At one point, Tianna tried to reproduce the pattern on a particular cricket's back and in so doing realized it wasn't unique: its cagemates all had similar markings. Marcy focused closely on the head. After drawing in features that she assumed were eyes, she mused, "I don't get how they can breathe. They don't have any nose." She considered the possibility that crickets might breathe through their mouths instead and looked more closely to double-check for a nose. Later, as she tried to work out how to attach legs to the body she had drawn, Marcy examined a real cricket and determined that the legs didn't simply "come out" of the sides but rather extended from underneath. It took some effort to get a good look at the insect's belly, and when she finally did, Marcy erased and adjusted her drawing, exclaiming, "There! That's how it looks!" (see Figure 7–2).

Afterward, Marcy described what it was like to shift her focus between the live crickets and her paper, explaining, "When you get a perfect glance, it's like, 'Oh, now I remember!'"

"And then what happens when you go to work on your drawing?" I asked.

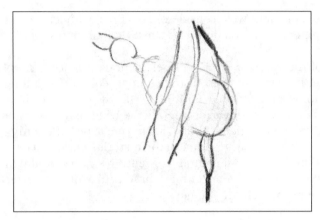

Figure 7–2   Marcy's sketch of the underside of a cricket

Laughing, she replied, "Oh, no! Now I forget!"

Other children have described the process in a similar way—they look at the object and "know" what it looks like but then "forget" when they go to draw. Over time, however, the back-and-forth between object and representation builds knowledge of specific details and relationships.

It is worth underscoring the role that the drawing played in Marcy's simple investigation of cricket anatomy. It was a tangible, visible description of what she had observed, a model she could compare with the actual animal. When she did compare, some aspects of the model bothered her. The legs were one: they didn't seem quite right. Improving the model required her to refine her understanding of the real insect, as well as to erase and remake lines.[2]

Drawings as Data

Professional scientists consider whether the data they have collected is reliable and whether it speaks to particular questions. Children can begin to grapple with such issues as well.

When children focus on phenomena that change over time, their drawings document these transformations. If questions arise, children can use their drawings as data. It is important in these instances for teachers to help children consider to what degree a particular drawing is reliable, for even when children draw from observation, they make deci-

2. For perspectives on how drawing and other modes of representing observations and ideas cause concepts to be refined or changed, see Ackerman (1990), Eisner (1983), and Jackman (1904).

sions about how precisely they will record particular information. For example, when Eliot drew a cricket, he began with the back. "I'm not going to do the exact design," he told me. "I'm just going to put the little lines, like that, for the design." Celia made a similar decision midway through drawing a budding twig. At first, she took care to count each bud and position it on her drawn twig precisely as it appeared on the actual one (see buds at far right). She apparently became fatigued with the effort, because she changed her approach midstream, sprinkling buds here and there until it looked like about enough (see Figure 7–3).

Sometimes, however, children are unaware of or don't recall the particular choices they made as they drew. Later, they may believe their drawings offer more information than they actually include. For example, when Aaron's class began to observe budding twigs, he pictured

Figure 7–3   Celia's drawing of a budding twig

his on a nine-by-twelve-inch sheet of drawing paper. His drawn twig ran nearly the full length of the paper. The following week, he used an eleven-by-fourteen-inch sheet instead. Once again, his drawn twig ran nearly the full length. Reviewing the record he had made, Aaron placed the two drawings side by side and assumed the twig had grown. In such instances, teachers can gently raise questions about what the record shows for sure and what data it may lack.

Teachers can also help children think through how to keep track of particular information that might later prove important. I did so with Aaron, who not only thought his twig had grown longer but believed it was sprouting more leaves as well. Aaron was comfortable with his impressions, ready to consider them facts and leave it at that. As a teacher committed to furthering his science education, I wanted Aaron to devise some way to confirm or disprove his "hypothesis" about the leaves. I wanted him to establish for sure whether the number was increasing.

Though Aaron had been watching his twig for some time, he didn't have the data to do this. He had made several detailed drawings, but in each had conveyed the twig's general leafiness rather than noting each and every leaf (see Figure 7–4). I challenged him to come up with a way to keep track of the exact number. He protested, asserting that this was unnecessary as he already knew he was right. Unmoved, I suggested he come up with a method of collecting the missing data that would not be unduly taxing. Aaron opted to approximate the number of leaves in his drawing, as he had been doing, and then to record the exact count in the corner of his picture. This approach let him focus on other details while he drew, yet equipped him to verify the statement he had made.

Attending to Ideas

In classrooms where drawing is a customary and respected mode of expression, children will use it to share and "play" with ideas—as did three first-grade friends who spent an independent work period at the guinea pig's cage. The guinea pig (the same classroom pet introduced in Chapter 3) was already a familiar sight. Still, he held interest for the girls, and as they watched him they chatted and drew. Their drawing, titled "Checkers' Food Route" (see Fig. 7–5) reveals their line of thought.

Checkers is outlined in profile with eye and ear indicated. Inside, as if seen with X-ray vision, are three large bones with knuckled ends. A channel runs back from the mouth, then divides. One path leads to a cul-de-sac, the other to a small, round structure. A second channel leads from the round structure to a more ill-defined, scribbled one. This is linked to the rear end of the guinea pig by a third channel. The guinea pig is sucking on its water bottle: the water it has swallowed is indicated

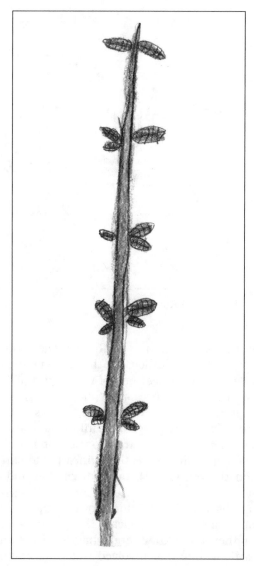

Figure 7–4 **Twig, drawn by Aaron**

by a broken line. Although I didn't oversee the creation of this drawing, the girls described it to me after they had finished. They noted that food and water go in at the mouth, then travel to the stomach (the round structure). In the stomach they are transformed into new material that travels (as indicated by a series of circles in the second channel) to yet

Figure 7–5   "Checkers' Food Route"

another part of the body where it is further changed. The girls were uncertain what this "place" was called, but thought that the material generated there traveled on to the rear end of the guinea pig's body where it
was somehow separated into "pee" and "poop," then eliminated.

These three girls, like many children, had been struck by the amount
of time the guinea pig spent eating and drinking, and also by the amount
of waste it produced. But what was the process that linked the two? What
could possibly be happening *inside* the guinea pig to explain what they
had observed on the outside? Through discussion and drawing, they
tried to figure it out.

As I review "Checkers' Food Route" now, the parallel between drawing and writing seems especially clear. The picture captures what the
girls knew, what they didn't know, and what they were uncertain of. The
process of creating it (one that involved watching, talking, and thinking, as well as drawing) allowed them to pull together information and
speculation, questions and answers, and integrate these in a "product"
that became a point of departure for further conversation and thought.

Sharing Ideas

The "food route" drawing was initiated by the children, but teachers can
also suggest (or require) that students portray ideas through drawing. The
process can prompt children to think more deeply about hidden or invis-

ible aspects of the world. To understand how it might, imagine what a child (or you) might draw in response to each of the following questions:

- "When the snail goes inside its shell, where, exactly, does it end up? How does it fit?"

- "What might be happening at the bottom of the pond?"

- "Can you show what the air is doing that would make that tree behave as it is?"

- "Given the changes you have seen in your plant over the last few days, what do you think it will look like tomorrow?"

In addition to giving the imagination a push, drawing can also make children's ideas available to others, as in the following example featuring a class that was divided about how to continue their study of some garden spiders that had produced large, silken egg sacs. Several children were deeply interested in these, speculated about their contents, and longed to know for sure what was happening inside. If only they could cut open the egg sacs and find out! I was prepared to honor their wish, but a few other members of the class objected. Even though they were not especially interested in the egg sacs, they didn't think it was right to alter them: it might hurt the eggs or babies.

In order to learn more about the range of ideas, hopes, and concerns that existed within the class, I asked all the children to show what they imagined might be in the egg sacs. They did so by sketching, in some cases adding a written word or statement. (See Figure 7–6.) When they were finished, I stapled all of the drawings onto a bulletin board and gave

Figure 7–6a   **Garden spider with egg sac by second-grade boy**

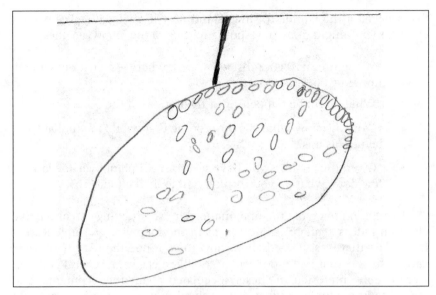

Figure 7–6b   **Child's notion of what is inside a spider's egg sac**

children time to study them. The pictures vividly revealed ideas, questions, and strong feelings, and helped children understand the reasoning of those with differing ideas. They were useful references as we worked to forge a solution to our standoff.

According to the *Standards*, "all science depends on the ultimate sharing and debating of ideas" (NRC 1996, 31–32). Children can draw their ideas as well as say them.

Clearing Up Confusions

Drawing does not exist as a distinct activity in a science classroom. Instead, children tend to look, think, gesture, draw, and discuss all at once. Drawing serves several purposes in this swirl of activity, and it is especially helpful in clarifying points and clearing up confusions. Often, children's pictures accomplish what their words alone cannot.

Tianna and Marcy, whose work with crickets I described earlier, incorporated drawing as they attempted to describe new discoveries. After exclaiming, "Oh, I see the mouth!" Marcy drew a sketch to explain what she had noticed. "It's like this part, and then those are here, and then maybe this would be its mouth? I just saw underneath, there's this little thing that they have." (See Figure 7–7.)

"Do you see this?" Tianna asked Marcy, pointing to her own drawing. "Well, then it's got these little things going dut! dut!" With each *dut*, she pointed to a tiny mark on her drawing of a cricket's face. Was it a nose, she wondered? Later, noting another miniature feature, she said, "Do you see it, Marcy? They're like a bunch of little itty-bitty lines. I'm going to draw that." She did so quickly, then held out her work. "I see it like this." (See Figure 7–8.)

"Oh," Marcy replied, continuing to refine her own drawing. "Oh, I see something different. This is what's on mine, like an arrowlike thing, a triangle. Then these black things right here." She added new marks to the cricket face on her paper. "Like, see? This is like the triangle."

"I see it like this," Tianna responded, also drawing. "I see it like a diamond, and then like, a thing coming down, and then the two black things."

"That's what I saw, too," Marcy replied, now convinced that although they were using different words, they were actually talking about the same feature.

Figure 7–7   Marcy's sketch of a cricket's head: note mouth

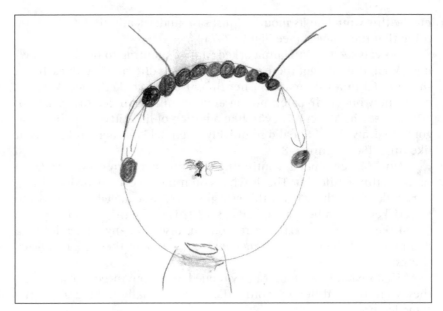

Figure 7–8   Tianna's sketch of a cricket's head

Support for Drawing

Teachers who believe that the writing process can help children learn tend to nurture that possibility in various ways. On a basic level, they make sure that the necessary tools are available and give children time to write. They expose children to new aspects of the writing craft through lessons or workshops and provide opportunities to practice, experiment, and develop skill. In addition, teachers encourage children to share works in progress and receive feedback. This model suggests possible ways to support children's drawing.

Find the Time

Some children love to draw and crave more time to do it. It isn't easy to find this time at school. Given all that is expected of classroom teachers, it is no wonder that many relegate drawing to the art room or to children's homes. When classroom time can be found, however, children who like to draw have a chance to pursue their special interest, and doing so can potentially lead them to other areas of involvement.

Karin and Suzanna loved to draw, and while they admired the box of feathers I made available during the early days of our study of birds, the brand-new box of pastels I had purchased for the art area really beguiled them. During a period in which I let students choose what they wanted to do, the girls decided to draw the feathers. After a while, I went over to see how things were going.

"Look what we did!" They eagerly held out beautiful pastel pictures.

Karen also held out a feather for me to inspect. "See? I showed how it looks on this side, and how it looks on the other. On this side the colors are really bright, but when you turn it over, they're not."

"And what did you have to do to show that?" I asked.

Karin showed me the many different pastels she had used, the places where she had mixed colors, and how she had muted colors by rubbing her paper with a tissue.

Day after day Karin and Suzanna took out the feathers. They rendered them with oil pastels, colored chalk, watercolors, and tempera paints (see Figure 7–9). Each time I checked in, they were full of

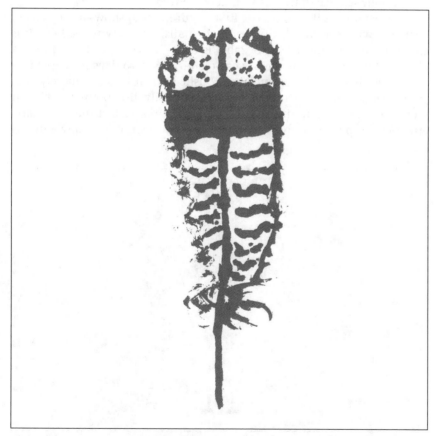

Figure 7–9   Painting of a turkey feather by eight-year-old girl

news about particular feathers as well as the qualities of the medium they'd used.

Children who love to draw will gravitate to it whenever they have the opportunity. A by-product of this passion can be new knowledge about whatever objects they represent. It may not be possible or productive to incorporate drawing to the same degree as writing, but it may pay to fit in more. For children like Karin and Suzanna, drawing is a path to closer acquaintance with the natural world.

Expect Varied Approaches

By showing drawings that are the result of painstaking realism, I don't mean to imply a general standard. A child can learn through the effort to create a close likeness, but other approaches are also of value. Children's intentions shape the products they create and are the lenses through which their science drawings should be viewed.

Two examples illustrate. The first (Figure 7–10a) shows a baby chick, complete with eye, wing, tiny comb, toenails, and downy feathers. It is carefully scaled: the "life size" label is entirely accurate. In contrast, a chick drawn by the same eight-year-old girl just two days later (see Figure 7–10b) bears little resemblance. Dashed off in haste, it merely suggests a baby bird. The second drawing could easily disappoint a teacher. It seems not to live up to the promise of the first nor reflect the same care, attention, or personal investment. In fact, however, it is simply a differ-

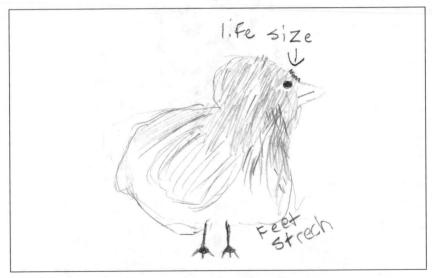

Figure 7–10a   Chloe's "life size" drawing of a chick

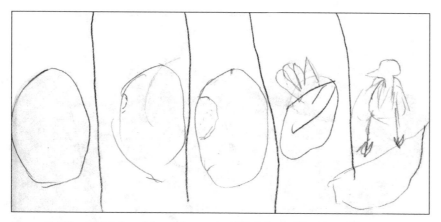

Figure 7–10b Chick hatching: sequence of quick sketches by Chloe, age eight

ent kind of record. It is the final "frame" in a sequence of sketches that capture a thrilling event: a chick actually hatching! Chloe, the child who drew it, could have focused more on the execution of her picture, but she would have had to tear herself away from the "real thing" in order to do so. There was no guarantee that another egg would hatch in her presence, so she wisely kept her eyes on the action and quickly captured its essence on paper.

Teachers who expect and appreciate a wide range of science drawings understand that children work with particular intentions or purposes in mind. Again, two very different drawings illustrate the point. Figure 7–11 depicts a single dragonfly wing as seen through a microscope. Hundreds of miniature, thornlike projections rim its cell-like divisions. The rest of the dragonfly is absent—unimportant for the time being. The drawing, like the written statement that accompanied it, reveals the mystery that captured the child's interest: ". . . the wings had little prickers and we do not know what they are for." Figure 7–12 is cartoonlike. Captioned "A cricket shedding," it shows a generic "bug" over time. In the first image, the cricket is half covered with its old skin, indicated with dark-colored pencil. In the second, the darkened area is reduced. Finally, we see the cricket entirely clothed in its pale, new skin, ever so slightly bigger than it was before. No effort was made to record a detailed likeness: that was not the point!

"I Can't Draw!"

I have worked with a number of children who find the very thought of drawing stressful. They would rather not put pencil to paper in that way. When required to draw, some of these children expend little energy on

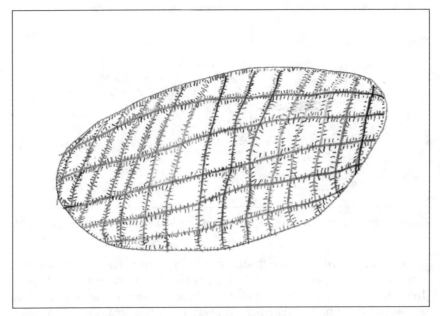

Figure 7–11   **Dragonfly wing, as seen through a microscope**

Figure 7–12   **"A cricket shedding," by second-grade Sylvie**

the task and stop as soon as they can. Others work diligently but are disappointed with the results. They resist sharing their drawings with others or referring to them later.

Nine-year-old Martin looked perpetually irritated as his class documented the growth of cabbage plants in the school garden. Each week he would measure and look at his plants, then dash off a drawing and hold it out to me, asking, "Is this good?" Almost before I could comment, he would snatch it back. "I don't like to draw," he told me during one such episode. "It's not that I'm not good at it, I don't even like it."

Martin liked and felt good at lots of things, among them baseball, reading, and adding large numbers. He accomplished these with ease and speed. Drawing from observation, however, went against the grain. It was slow. The standard to which he was working was elusive, difficult to attain. However, since he sometimes showed me his drawings and asked if I thought they were good, I suspected he longed for reassurance. Perhaps he also longed to be more skillful, so that his drawn records would better match what he had seen. However, he was so quick to snatch his drawings back and so adamant about not spending any more time than necessary on them that it was hard to help him gain that skill.

Charlie was another child for whom drawing in science class was problematic. Charlie moved to my school in the third grade, joining a group of children who were used to incorporating drawing in their science observations and experiments. A responsible and hardworking child, Charlie dutifully observed, discussed, and drew the insects, birds, and other things I required children to focus on. At the end of each period, he would look appraisingly at his paper, crumple it up, and throw it away.

This concerned me; I viewed his finished drawings as valuable information that might come in handy later. More important, the crumpling revealed his discouragement, dissatisfaction, and sense of inadequacy. He didn't feel his work measured up. On occasion, that kind of self-assessment spurs a child to renewed effort and accomplishment. In Charlie's case, that outcome seemed unlikely. I decided to keep an eye on Charlie whenever I required drawing as part of science work and to intercept his next attempt to discard his record.

The next time I saw Charlie ball up his sketch and toss it in the trash, I retrieved the paper. Charlie noticed. "It wasn't good," he maintained.

I didn't challenge his judgment, instead asking, "Would you mind if I keep it for a while? I'm interested in the plants we're studying, and your drawing shows me a lot about how this one looks."

I repeated this maneuver on several other occasions, each time smoothing the discarded paper, asking permission to keep it, and making a specific comment about its content. "This drawing has the colors of the real flower, and that information is important for us to remember," I'd say, or, "This drawing will remind me of the way the finch holds its head when it drinks."

After a while Charlie stopped wadding up his drawings and started bringing them to me instead. "Do you want to keep this?" he'd ask as he approached—and indeed I did. Eventually, he began keeping them himself.

Children look to teachers to learn what we find important, worthy, and correct. The fact that I focus on science drawings as valuable records containing interesting information comes as a relief to some of my students. Freed from the imagined burden of having to create aesthetically pleasing pictures that look just like the real thing, they can focus on the subject at hand and learn about it through drawing. They can respect their own work for the same reasons I do and perhaps even gain enough skill and comfort with drawing to take more pleasure in it. When children don't respond even to this more easygoing approach to drawing, it may be important to emphasize other modes of inquiry and record keeping.

Help Children Learn the Language

I've noted that the sloppy or incomplete appearance of a particular science drawing may belie the role that creating it played in helping a child to learn. That said, I also acknowledge that the degree of drawing skill a child possesses is important. Again, I make a parallel with writing. The greater our command of either craft, the more precisely we can express our observations and ideas. The more skillful we are, the more possible it is to communicate complex understandings or explore topics in sophisticated ways.

With this in mind, I try not to gloss over the frustrations children encounter as they draw. Instead, I acknowledge the problems they face and help them look for solutions. Many times, it takes little work on my part other than "hanging in there" with children as they experiment with ways to make line and color depict what they see.

For example, in the midst of drawing an ivy plant that trailed over the edge of its pot, Sasha began testing various shades of green in the lower-left corner of his paper. He judged his first attempt "way too light." He proceeded through the supply of colored pencils, and eventually found a shade that satisfied him. He then began drawing the leaves while looking intently at the potted ivy. Stopping to inspect his paper, he blurted, "What did I do that for? I was thinking about something else and I just drew a line!"

"How did you want it to go?" I asked, concerned at his frustration.

"Over here," Sasha pointed, crossing out the offending line. He outlined the stem in brown and filled it with several shades of carefully tested green (see Figure 7–13). He commented on how much his drawing varied from the actual ivy in its pot: "This looks like a balloon!" he said in dismay.

"Did you want it to look different?" I asked. Sasha grimaced: of course he did! Thinking it might help him to identify a specific discrepancy, I asked if his drawn pot looked different from the real one in some way.

Figure 7–13 Sasha's drawing of a potted plant

"It doesn't have any white dots in it," Sasha quickly replied, referring to the flecks scattered across the actual soil.

"Maybe your drawing doesn't have to show everything, just the main things," I offered, hoping to convey support for his effort and keep the difficulty of the task from spiraling unreasonably.

"Well, that *is* a main thing!" Sasha retorted, unmoved.

Despite his dissatisfaction, Sasha continued his drawing. He focused next on a cluster of leaves. Holding a leaf between thumb and forefinger he mused, "The leaves are kind of like a triangle shape." He managed to capture the shape quite closely as he outlined each leaf in pencil, but as he compared his drawing with plant I could sense his frustration growing again.

"I'm showing something I noticed on the leaves," he said, making marks with a green pencil.

"What's that?" I asked.

"These little line things," he replied, pointing out the veins. He added veins to each leaf in the group, finally turning his paper sideways and cross-hatching the leaf on the bottom. He wasn't happy with the effect. "The lines got messed up," he complained. "I just don't like the crossing. That's not even real."

I asked Sasha which one of the leaves on his picture looked most real to him. Pointing in turn to each leaf in the cluster of three, he offered, "This one [the top leaf] has the best shape. This [the middle leaf] has the best lines. This [the bottom-right leaf] has an off shape. There's too much point in it."

Essentially, Sasha gave himself a drawing lesson, trying out a different technique on each leaf and comparing the results to the actual plant. His finished picture documents the range of approaches he tried, culminating with the two leaves shown nearest the pot. Children often

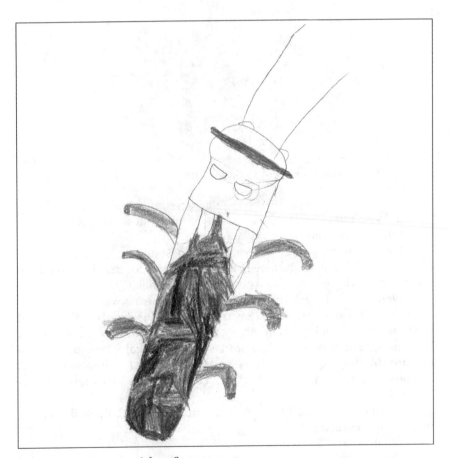

Figure 7–14a   Irene's cricket: first attempt

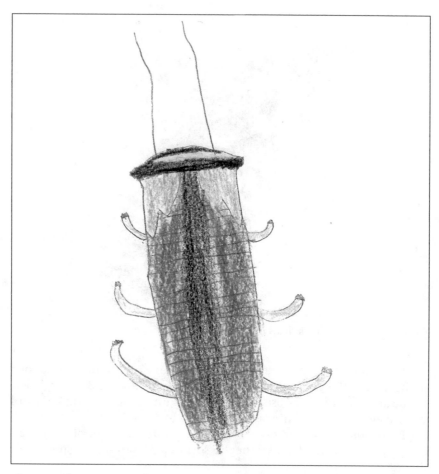

Figure 7–14b   Irene's cricket: second attempt

develop drawing skill in this way, trying different approaches and appraising the results, experimenting until satisfied with the match.

Children also turn to one another for instruction. Sometimes, they study someone else's drawing as they continue to experiment and to observe the actual object. Irene's work shows what can result. Her first drawing of a house cricket depicts the striking pattern on its back with curved, interlocking bands of color (see Figure 7–14a). Her second, which portrays it differently and more realistically (see Figure 7–14b), perhaps owes something to her study of a friend's drawing of the cricket (see Figure 7–15).

Figure 7–15   **Stephanie's drawing of a cricket**

I facilitate this kind of learning when I can. For example, Lisa, one of the girls in the group I used as an example in Chapter 3, struggled as she began to record her observations of the guinea pig. Erasing her third start, she exclaimed, "Guinea pigs are hard to draw!"

Beth pointed to her own picture and offered a tip. "I found an easy way," she said, "It's like they're sort of a shape—like a spread-out shape."

I restated Beth's comment slightly, hoping to provide Lisa with a new way to think about her own work. "So when you start to draw, Beth, you try to get the body shape first."

Beth nodded. "Then I add the ears and all."

"You've got the curved shape of his back now," I remarked to Lisa. She continued her outline, satisfied with the way it portrayed the real animal.

Draw with the Children

I make it a point to draw with my students. Like many of them, I don't find the task of rendering objects or organisms easy, and I'm not always satisfied with the results. It can be affirming for children to see that this is just "the nature of the beast." Even grown-ups have to work at it. Sometimes, children have been impressed with some aspect of my drawing. When that happens, I share what I understand about what I did, not as the right way but as a possible way, one that anyone else may try. Likewise, I ask about their approaches and try my hand at copying.

One such occasion occurred as the general hubbub that accompanied the sudden emergence of a butterfly was dying down. The whole class had gathered for the big event, and gradually children began returning to other activities. I stayed on with a small group, but instead of focusing on the children's work, I took up crayons and began to draw alongside them.

Daren and Anya were especially interested in my work. They noted my use of the crayon sharpener on the box with great excitement: it was a tool they had not been aware of. At various points they commented admiringly on my picture and took turns trying out a particular color I used. Jacob, who had been working entirely in pencil, also noted my work and switched to crayon. An animated, experimental attitude took hold in the group. Each of us tried things out, inspected one another's drawings, and selected new things to copy.

"I like that."

"This doesn't work so well for me."

"How did you get it to go that way?"

Conduct Drawing Workshops

Informal workshops where the process of drawing is explicitly discussed and demonstrated are yet another avenue for helping children develop their skill. These can be improvised or scheduled in advance. Be sure to ask children questions about how they achieved particular effects or results, inquire about what they are struggling with, demonstrate new options, and encourage imitation.

I planned such a workshop after a wildlife rehabilitator visited my classroom with two live owls. In the days that followed, children tried to learn more. They listened to recorded owl calls, read about the birds, and also tried to draw them. Jalisa could really do it! The owls in her pictures looked remarkably like those that had visited our class. Other children voiced their admiration and also their dissatisfaction with their own efforts. Even when they used photographs as models, something about their owls looked a little funny. Jalisa demonstrated her technique on chart paper, explaining how she made the top of the head a little flat, and drew the beak with nearly parallel lines. Her classmates followed her advice with good results.

8 Reviewing Children's Work

Classroom teachers are continually evaluating and planning, deciding from one moment to the next where to steer the class and how best to help individual children. We base these decisions on information we gather while watching our students, interacting with them, and examining their products. Reviewing the records children make as they explore the world around them can help us establish what they are learning and imagine how they might further their work. Some examples of those records, completed by children aged five through eleven and providing insights into their ideas, accomplishments, and priorities, are presented below. My annotations highlight some of the observations reflected in the drawings, translate invented spellings, and identify qualities or approaches that are common at a particular age.

Teachers who are unfamiliar with work of this kind may feel unsure how to respond when a child proudly presents a finished paper. Looking it over, we may see careful attention to detail but also note errors and omissions. The emphasis on accuracy and objectivity that we have come to associate with science can make us especially aware of "mistakes." One way to broaden our focus is to use drawings, written records, and other products as windows through which we can glimpse bits of what a child knows and wonders about. We can also use them to spark conver-

The *Standards* urge teachers to choose assessment strategies that "support the development of students' understanding and nurture a community of science learners." Teachers can monitor the development of understanding as students work (NRC 1996, 30, 32). Reviewing drawings and written records such as the ones shown here accomplishes these aims.

sations that may deepen understanding or generate the next step in an ongoing investigation. I avoid "correcting" these records. I especially try not to add marks or comments that shift the focus away from the central topic of study and on to spelling, punctuation, or grammar. When my appraisal of a particular piece of work indicates I should teach or review specific writing skills, I make a note to do so at another time.

Examples to Review

In order to appreciate children's work and use it to inform our teaching, we must recognize what it contains. This takes practice. I find it useful to review selections with other teachers. Colleagues often note details I have missed or share insights that enrich my perspective. You may wish to review and evaluate the examples presented here before considering my interpretations. You can also imagine what next step might be fruitful for the child who made each and think of responses that might encourage further investigation.

DANNY'S GUINEA PIG OBSERVATION RECORD

Danny (age five years, seven months) has captured the oblong shape of the guinea pig's body. He has included a head and four legs and has shown that the guinea pig has no tail. Within the body Danny has drawn the heart, stomach, and liver (parts he cannot see, but that he explained "are on the inside"). A zigzag line begins at the guinea pig's chest, surrounds the tiny head, then continues on along its back. Despite the color (blue and yellow), it may represent fur. Children at this age sometimes mix designs, fantastic colors, and smiling faces with actually observed details. The four legs of Danny's guinea pig don't quite connect to the body. Though many five-year-olds would not leave such a gap, some will.

Danny's writing reflects his understanding that lots of letters can be used to express an idea; however, he has not used letters that relate to his verbal description. His text, "HEJUPSVRAN," may be copied from the flip chart—it approximates "He jumps and runs."

Danny's ability to focus on drawing and writing during this session may well have been aided by the fact that he had already had several chances to look at and hold the guinea pig. He was also able to talk informally with classmates as he worked, an aid to thinking. Kindergarten is an important time for children to be gathering experience and developing language to describe their world. Teachers responding to these discussions do well to remember that young children's explanations and reasoning about cause and effect will reflect their immaturity.

Name of Scientist __Danny__

I looked at _____

A picture of what I saw

I noticed HE ___ OBSVRAN

Figure 8–1   Danny's guinea pig

MANDY'S GUINEA PIG OBSERVATION RECORD

Mandy (age six years, eight months) has shown the shape of the guinea pig's body and head with more accuracy than a younger child would. She has also included many details, such as short legs, feet with toes, a black eye, a pink rounded ear, the pattern of brown and white fur, and a mouth and nostril. (Six-year-olds tend to make drawings that are more detailed and realistic than those they made at five, but happy faces and decorations are sometimes still included.) She has scribbled brown fur and quickly outlined and partially filled in the log in the guinea pig's cage. This "dashed-off" quality is common at her age.

Mandy has written, "It eats the log. He jumps." These statements describe the most notable behavior of the guinea pig during this session. On an earlier record, Mandy also included her reactions to the animal: "He is cute. I like him." Mandy's writing, like that of many six-year-olds, combines upper- and lowercase letters, invented and conventional spellings, and letter reversals. I accepted these without comment since they occur in the writings of many young children. With time and instruction they are usually outgrown.

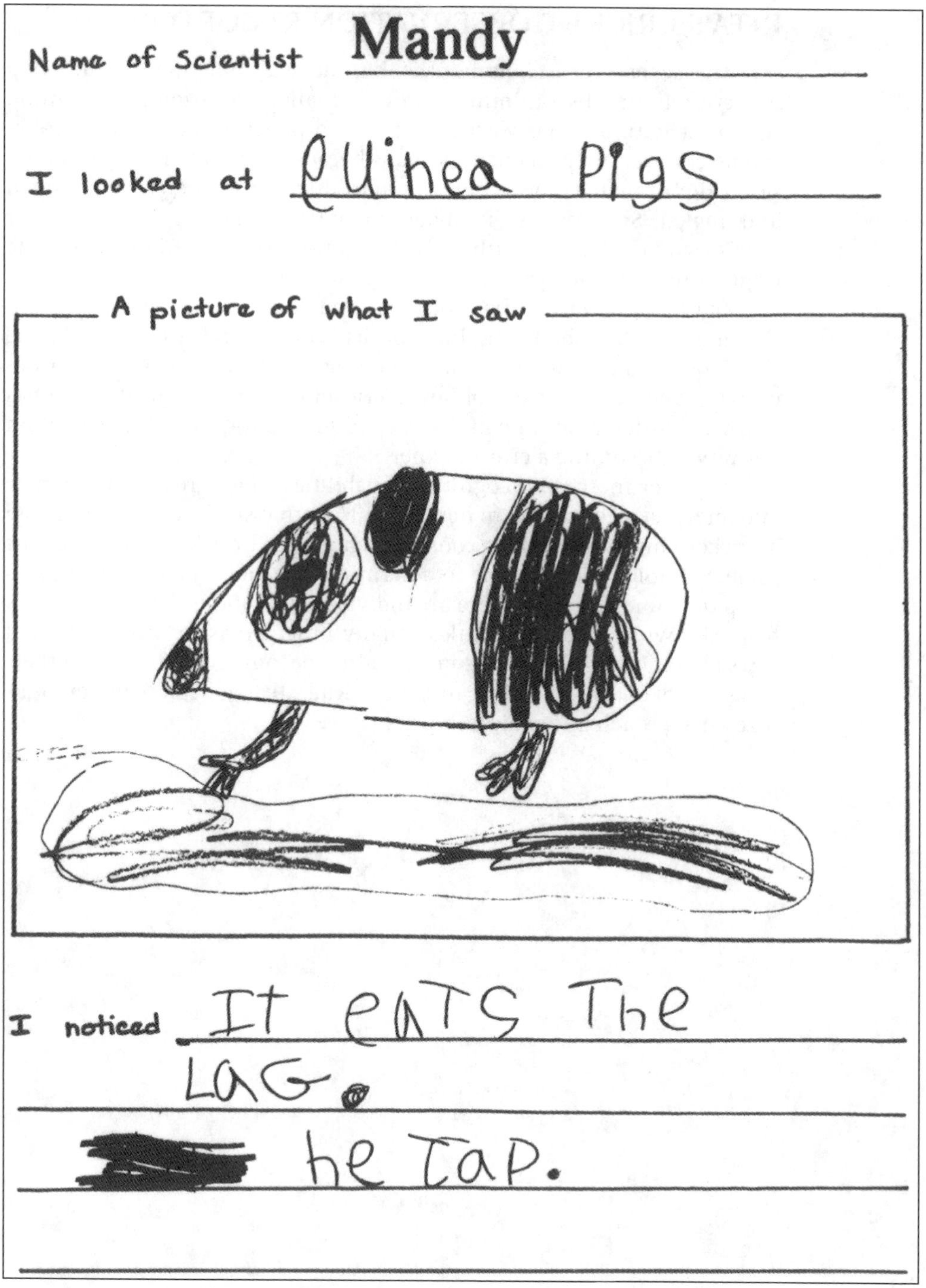

Name of Scientist   **Mandy**

I looked at $\underline{euinea \ PigS}$

_____ A picture of what I saw _____

I noticed   IT eATS The
LAG.
~~ he Tap.

Figure 8–2   Mandy's guinea pig

RITA'S CRICKET OBSERVATION RECORD

Rita (age seven years, eight months) has made a small, detailed drawing of a cricket after discontinuing an even smaller first attempt (shown on the lower left). She has worked entirely in pencil rather than in color. (Some children prefer pencil, perhaps because of their interest in precision.) Her drawing shows the front and hind legs of the cricket, jointed and angled. She has also included abdominal segments, several other divisions on the body, mouth parts, two tail-like cerci, and two antennae originating near the eye.

Rita has written: "It had four legs and two little things up in front that it ate with. It had little lines on its bottom, and it chirped for me and I looked and saw little wings moving." It is evident from both her drawing and her discovery of how a cricket eats and chirps that she has devoted considerable time and attention to this inquiry. Rita is well on her way to becoming a cricket expert.

With her increasing cognitive capabilities, she is ready to organize and interpret information in new ways. Now that she has discovered how a cricket chirps, she might consider whether all crickets chirp, or just some. She might also be able to determine whether all chirping crickets chirp the same way, or if there are individual variations. With a teacher's help, she will be able to think of many other areas to investigate and ways of doing so. At this age some children become so engrossed in their amassing of details, they lose direction. Rita's teacher can help her organize an approach and maintain perspective.

Rita's observation

date: August, 29th

I looked at A criket.

___ A picture of what I saw ___

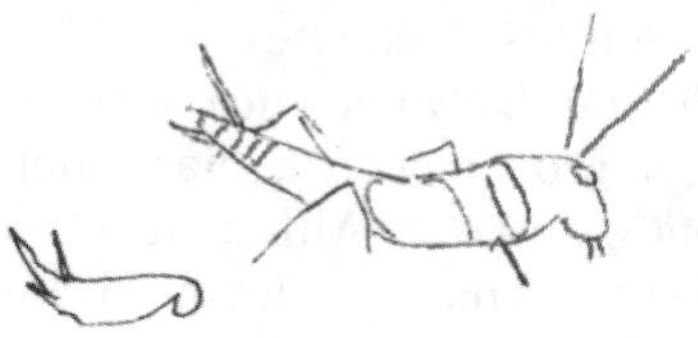

Here are some things I noticed:
it had 4 legs and to little things
up in front that it ate with.
it had little lines on it's bottom.
and it chirped for me and I looked
and saw little wings moveing.

Figure 8–3   Rita's cricket

RAY'S SPICE FINCH OBSERVATION RECORD

This drawing by Ray (age eight years, six months) shows the spice finch perched in its food dish, with front toes over the edge and back toe opposing the front. Wing, tail, and head are shaded brown; the breast is covered with tiny brown markings. The fat beak is a characteristic Ray and his classmates have come to associate with birds in the finch family. Ray's picture exhibits his developing capacity to create realistic drawings based on close attention to detail. He can benefit from focused instruction in art as well as from opportunities to experiment with paper and pencil.

Ray has written: "I noticed a pattern about the finches. That I think the male goes out and eats some food then either gets a piece of grass and goes back in or he just goes back in." Ray has taken care to use the term *male*, rather than *father*, when referring to the finch. His spontaneous identification of a pattern provides an excellent point of departure for further, focused observation. Identifying patterns is important in understanding bird behavior and in other science work as well. Ways in which the habits and social structure of birds parallel and diverge from that of human families interests Ray and his classmates.

Parents and teachers understandably become concerned about spelling and punctuation as children grow older. Ray has generalized the use of apostrophes, writing *go's, git's,* and *ete's.* Although this will be important to clarify in a separate exercise, creating a focus on apostrophes here might detract from his important observation of a pattern of behavior.

At this age he can design and carry out simple investigations, keep records, and use reference books with more independence than he could at seven. He still needs a teacher's help to organize and carry out his research.

Ray's _____ observation

date: ___5/4_____

I looked at ___SPISE finchis_____

_____A picture of what I saw_____

Here are some things I noticed:

I notist a Patar about The finchis
That I Thing The male Go's
Out and ete's som food Than
ethor Git's a Dese of Gras
and Go's Bake in oT He Jost
Go's Bake in.

Figure 8–4   Ray's spice finch

SUSAN'S NEST OBSERVATION RECORD

Susan (age nine years, two months) has drawn a nest built into a forking branch. She has blended colored pencils to show the shade of the nest and tree bark. Rather than attempting a literal depiction of each leaf, she has sketched in green and brown lines to give the effect of many leaves.

Susan's writing reflects the different senses she has employed while exploring the nest. Her curious observation, "It is strange how the leaves stayed green and they are dry," seems to reveal a preconception that leaves fade or turn color as they dry out. Susan has already amassed a wealth of information about the world from her own experience, from books, and from television. Applying this information to new situations and testing what she has heard and read against her own direct observations are habits to encourage.

In categorizing an observation as "strange," Susan has taken the first step toward raising a question to research. She is quite capable of extending her work and designing an investigation that might lead her to learn more about her surprising observation. She could compare the leaves in this nest with other dry leaves or gather some fresh leaves and note how they change over time. Continuing to observe this nest and noting whether the color of the dry leaves or the "fresh" smell persists might also deepen her understanding. Though a teacher may perceive "holes" in her procedures or reasoning, Susan will learn from solving problems as they arise.[1]

1. Nest collecting is regulated by federal law, as noted on page 92.

Susan's observation

date: feb. 26

I looked at a nest

A picture of what I saw

Here are some things I noticed:
it is soft it smells fresh it
is strange how the leaves stayed
green and ~~fell~~ they are dry. it
has a lot of detail it has birch
bark and pine neetles and
sticks. it is pretty small.

Figure 8–5 Susan's nest

ETHAN'S SPICE FINCH OBSERVATION RECORD

Ethan's record shows that he has paid attention both to the appearance and behavior of the finches. In his drawing this ten-year-old boy has used lines to suggest feathers, and he has given the birds humanlike eyes. He has shown both birds in profile (erasing a first attempt to draw the finch in the nest basket, face on). Many children find side views of animals easiest to manage. Ethan's drawing suggests interaction and activity.

In observing "that the top of the head goes right to the beak without going down," Ethan has discovered for himself a characteristic that distinguishes finches from many other birds. Aspects of nesting behavior have also been noted both in his illustration and his writing. "One is usually in the nest, the nest has a lot of grass in it, I think that they're going to have babies soon."

Ethan could extend this research in several directions. Many children his age enjoy sorting, classifying, and listing information. He could classify the birds he knows according to some observable feature, such as beak shape. He could also explore the birds' behavior further. (Do the birds take turns in the nest, or does one bird do most of the sitting? Do the birds select any other materials besides grass for the nest?) Since children reveal many of their ideas on these records, teachers often find the records useful springboards for discussions. Ethan's prediction that the birds are going to have babies, for example, might lead to an interesting discussion and a plan for monitoring the nest.

The study of bird behavior is well suited to fieldwork. Though fieldwork is important and enjoyable at any age, many older children seem to thrive on it. They are energetic, capable of keeping track of equipment (with occasional reminders), and often enjoy being outside for extended periods. Ethan and his classmates spent quite a bit of time observing birds both outdoors and through the classroom windows. He devised a way to record different flight patterns in a notebook and associated some of these with particular species.

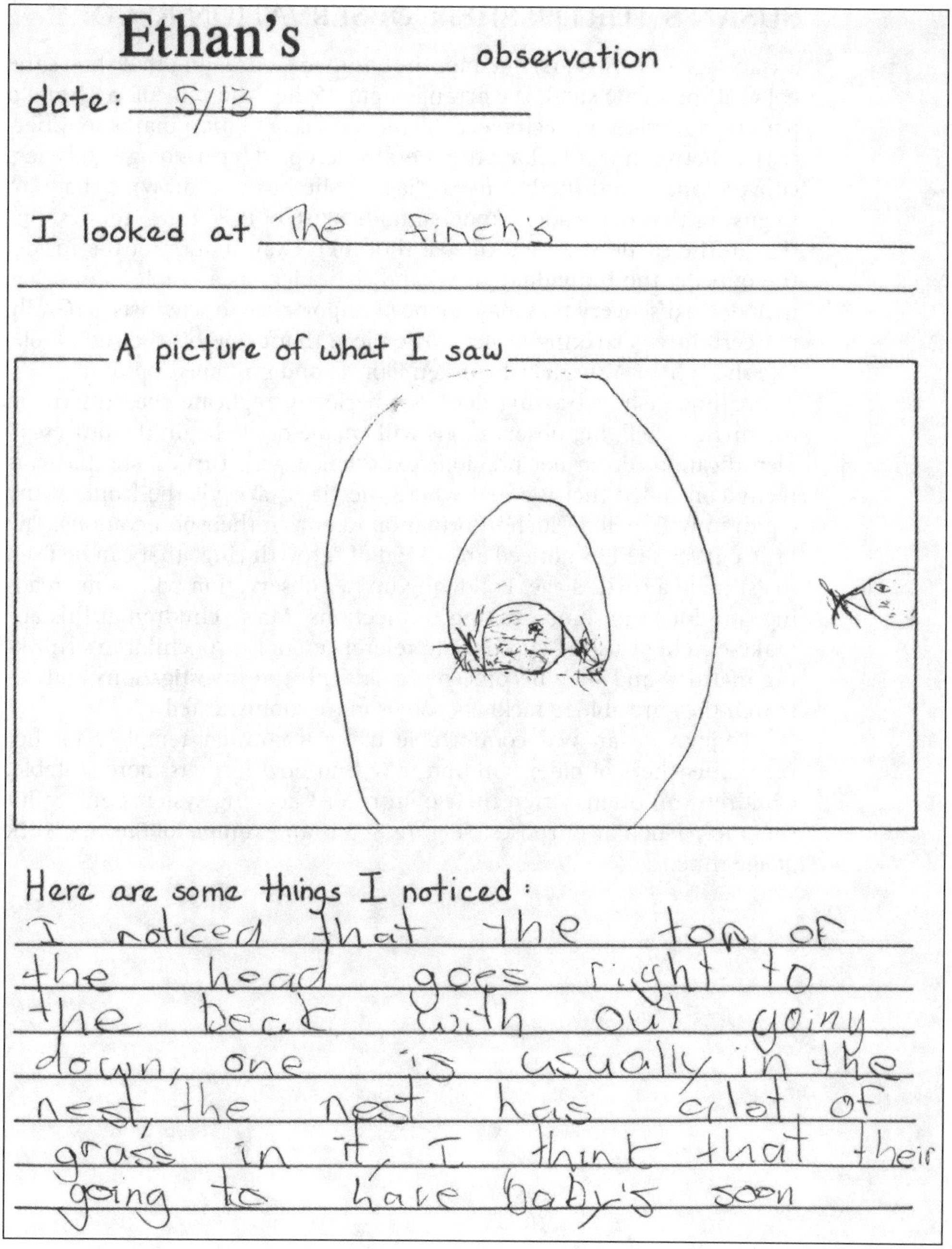

Ethan's _____ observation

date: ___5/13_____

I looked at _The   finch's_____

_____

_____ A picture of what I saw _____

Here are some things I noticed:
I noticed that the top of
the head goes right to
the beak with out going
down, one is usually in the
nest, the nest has alot of
grass in it, I think that their
going to have baby's soon

Figure 8–6   Ethan's finch

SUSAN'S TURTLE SHELL OBSERVATION RECORD

Susan (age eleven years, one month) has made a drawing that shows the color of the turtle shell, the arrangement of the different "pieces," and a pattern or design on each piece. She has used quotation marks to differentiate between words that are generally accepted terminology and a less conventional word she has used ("jags"); she has also drawn a diagram to ensure that her readers understand her use of this term. Her description of the turtle shell indicates a thorough examination of the inside, the outside, the individual parts, and the object as a whole. Susan has included a discovery that may not be of importance to scientists generally but certainly is striking to her: "The piece that came off the shell looks like the U.S. of A. with a shrunken Florida and no Cape Cod!"

Although her drawing does not perfectly replicate the pattern on the turtle's shell, her observations will enable her to begin the process of identification. From her previous experience with turtles, she has correctly concluded that the end where the "jags" arise is the front. Many children will include such information to enrich their observations. The little curves she has noticed are a kind of "growth ring" that can be used to estimate a turtle's age. Following up her observation with some reading could lead to some exciting connections. Many children at this age make excellent use of appropriate reference books. As children's thinking matures and they become more skillful, the investigations and research they are able to tackle becomes more sophisticated.

Though Susan was comfortable using a familiar template for her record, teachers of older children may find new formats more suitable. Children can often design their own record-keeping systems and tailor them to particular purposes. (Figure 8–5 is an example of Susan's work at age nine.)

Susan's _____ observation

date: 1/18 _____

I looked at ___One of the turtle shells.___
___and some of the pieces from the shells,___

_____ A picture of what I saw _____

Here are some things I noticed:
The shell has the spine of the turtle on the inside,
there are "jags" rising up from the shell:
in the front (where the turtle's head would be)
it is raised up. The piece that came off the
shell looks like the U.S. of A. with a shrunken
Florida and no cape cod! the brown parts
have lots of little curves.

Figure 8–7   Susan's turtle shell

What About Children with Learning Challenges?

Science work can be interesting, fun, and exciting for all children, including those who face extra challenges at school. Throughout this book, children with specific learning disabilities, sensitivities, or special needs have been shown observing, investigating, and discussing ideas with teachers and classmates. Carrie (see Chapter 1) approached me as I cleaned up pieces of a broken bottle and said, "I was wondering, maybe we could make sea glass." Alex (see Chapter 2) taught himself to draw guinea pigs by studying a classmate's picture. Angie (see Chapter 5) discovered the circular ears on a frog, later getting her classmates to join her in figuring out how a frog's tongue works. Ricky and Patrick (see Chapter 6) sifted through a bag of potting soil to see if they could find support for their hypothesis about the origin of the weeds that had appeared in their tulip pots. The care and attention Phillip devoted to recording twig observations (see Figure 8–14 in this chapter) inspired similar attention and care from many classmates.

Diversity within a science classroom is a valuable asset, especially when children work together. Many observations contribute to the collective store of knowledge, and a wide range of skills enables a group to identify and pursue questions, solve problems, and express understanding. When science work is broad and varied, children (including those with learning disabilities or other challenges) have the greatest opportunity to grow and to contribute to the growth of others. I am struck by how often the child who struggles with writing can reveal a wealth of interest and information through her drawing, movement, or music. The one who seems most ill at ease within the confines of the classroom may be the very child who emerges as a leader during fieldwork, able to locate the tiniest of wildflowers, sidestep poison ivy, or lend support to a classmate afraid of thunder, wasps, or snakes.

One way to maximize learning opportunities for all children is to provide many avenues for learning and expression in school. It is equally important to provide encouragement and support for children when they attempt work that proves frustrating or difficult or when they make the inevitable comparisons between their products or abilities and those of classmates. Children with learning disabilities or other challenges can feel confused when trying to follow a class discussion, frustrated when they can't read their own records, or concerned about the way their work looks on display. It may be difficult to retrieve the words, facts, or figures that would make their ideas clear to others. As Noelle, age nine, told her teacher, "I think my brain is like a rubber ball. The information goes in, but then it just bounces back out."

We can help by creating a community in which each child's work is acknowledged and used. Experimenting with the parameters of activities and assignments is also important. If the goal is to get everyone doing science, then obstacles to participation must be removed. Sometimes this is straightforward: instructions can be pictured as well as spoken, keyboarding can replace handwriting, a quiet time or workplace can be found, a bilingual child can translate for one new to the language of instruction. In other instances it is difficult to know what will enable a particular child, and teachers must experiment with accommodations.

Some Ideas for Differentiating Science Work

The basic approach I've suggested in this book asks children to pay sustained, close attention to classmates and to the objects being studied. It also emphasizes discussion, drawing, writing, and planning. These activities are the very ones that some children find most taxing. How can teachers ease the way? Outlining the full range of challenges that can impact science learning and identifying ways to address them is beyond the scope of this book. However, a few ideas may orient readers to the possibilities.

Focusing Attention

Many children have difficulty focusing their attention during a science lesson or when working independently at the science table. They may look briefly at an object on display then get up and move to another activity, they may look out the window instead of at the materials they've been given, or they may be distracted by activity elsewhere in the room. Observing—the first step in many science activities—will challenge these children. It may help them if we can define the task in more concrete terms: "Observe means you look closely. When a scientist looks closely at an object, she looks at the top and the bottom and at the sides—all around! A scientist looking at this shell would even have to look at the inside! When you've had a good look at all of the parts of this shell—its top, bottom, and sides—then you'll be ready to draw what you've noticed."

Initially, we can be available to guide children's inquiries, making sure that children both understand what it means to look closely and are able to do it. Later, children can monitor their own work using a checklist. Other activities may also need to be defined specifically. "A good description of an animal tells at least three things about how it looks. One thing you can look for is color. What colors do you see on this caterpillar?"

Not all children will be able to attend to an experiment, observe, or develop a drawing or description for the same amount of time. One seven-year-old may work for forty minutes. Another may have trouble focusing for five. Defining and limiting a task helps some children who have a tendency to "flit." By providing them with specific things to look for and report on and a checklist or other system to let them know when they are done, we enable children to work with greater independence and do work of a higher quality, extending their ability to participate in the class.

Keeping Records

Records can be written, typed, or tape-recorded by a child, or a teacher or a classmate can take dictation. Any system that allows information to be remembered and shared is a good one. When children tackle their own record keeping, there are many ways to make their task more manageable. When repeated observations are made of the same subject, checklists (which children can help us develop) can simplify the process of recording information. (For example, the class can list or draw pictures of bird behaviors on a page the teacher can copy. Children can then underline or check those seen.) Words or phrases that have come up during class discussions can be listed on a chart or "word wall" or written on a spiral-bound deck of index cards. These can be posted or stored at the science table, available for children to copy. Science studies are often laden with new terminology. Even children without academic challenges benefit when labels or charts containing relevant vocabulary are displayed. For children who struggle with writing or word retrieval, this is especially important.

Individualizing expectations for written work is also important. Some eight-year-olds can easily turn out a multipage report about their mealworms or magnets; others work hard to manage one sentence. We can tailor children's assignments to their abilities. Some children who have difficulty with written or spoken language express themselves more readily through drawing or gesture. Children will employ these modes during science lessons if they are valued as legitimate ways to share information.

Contributing During Meetings

Children often hesitate to share information or ideas during science meetings. Some are shy by temperament, while others falter because reading, speaking, or remembering poses challenges. We can help children who struggle to read their own writing by providing verbal cues, special notations, or a typed copy. Teachers can also supply sentence patterns to make written or spoken language more manageable. Some children are more comfortable talking about what they've noticed than they are reading from their written records, while other children are just the opposite. Rehearsing contributions ahead of time can benefit both groups. Some children have trouble recalling or articulating ideas and discoveries, especially when they feel the pressure of time or many eyes upon them. Conducting meetings in a leisurely way and assisting with recall or retrieval can support these students, as in this example:

ELLEN D.: I remember, Paul, that when you were looking at that blue feather the other day, you noticed something unusual about it. Remember when you held it up to the light? What happened?

PAUL: I don't remember.

ELLEN D.: It was the color . . .

PAUL: It changed!

ELLEN D.: You showed me how the color changes from blue to brown.

Sometimes a child's oral delivery of information is confusing to classmates. This can be embarrassing and frustrating for both speaker and listeners. We can come to the rescue by restating ideas in a way that enables the child to communicate more clearly and enables classmates to appreciate the student's good thinking. Our choice of words at such a juncture is important. Ideally, it should clarify what the child has expressed in a way that credits rather than corrects. I attempted this with nine-year-old Carol in the aftermath of a bird-watching trip:

CAROL: We saw those—you know—not the ducks but the other ones.

ELLEN D.: You saw the geese?

CAROL: Yes. We saw the geese, and when that man put the food out, they were eating it, but not the ducks. They just stood there. But after, we saw the ducks eating. I was thinking maybe they have to wait. The other ones go first.

ELLEN D.: I see. Your idea is that when it's time to eat, the geese eat first. When the geese are finished, the ducks can take a turn.

CAROL: Yes. Like they're the bosses.

ELLEN D.: The geese are the bosses.

When we recognize and help children express what they know, we enable them to contribute during meetings and we ease the embarrassment and frustration that otherwise might occur.

More Examples to Review

In science as well as in other areas of the curriculum, the particular interests, strengths, and needs of different children shape their approach and products. The following observation records were completed by children who participated in all aspects of the science programs in their classrooms but who confronted particular obstacles to learning as they did so. Each received ongoing services to address special needs that had been identified by teachers and evaluators. My annotations indicate each child's age, note specific issues, and suggest possible accommodations.

* * *

SETH'S TWIG OBSERVATION RECORD

Seth (age six years, three months) is a child with significant gross and fine motor challenges. He finds writing and drawing difficult. Here he has observed a twig and shown the pattern of its branches and the jar that held the twig. He chose a brown pencil to indicate the color of the bark. The encircled number one indicates that this record is the first in a series: Seth and his classmates forced twigs and looked at them many times over the course of several weeks, maintaining ever-growing collections of notes and drawings to review.

During informal discussions with his classmates or his teachers, Seth shared far more about his observations and predictions than he could convey with pencil. Given the intense effort Seth had to expend to produce drawings or text (and their limited effectiveness in communicating his understanding), it was important to relieve the pressure to do so while keeping Seth involved in the study. Therefore, I varied my approach—taking dictation as Seth provided information, having Seth record his own observations, and asking Seth to draw what he noticed without writing.

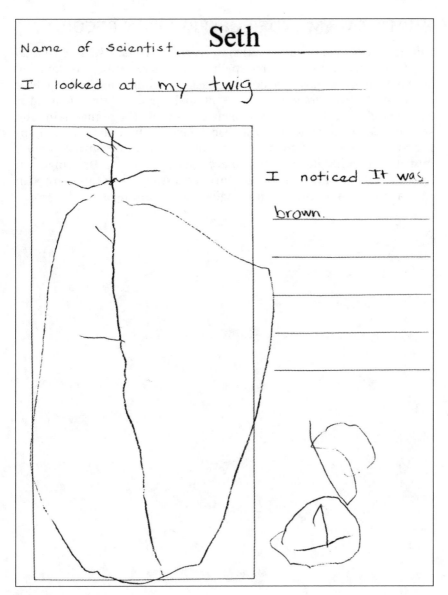

Name of scientist **Seth**

I looked at my twig

I noticed It was brown.

Figure 8–8 Seth's twig

KURT'S SALAMANDER OBSERVATION RECORD

Kurt (age eight years, eight months) works to overcome visual-perceptual problems that affect reading and spelling (the *d/b* reversals, for example). He has written, "It has a line down its back and orange and black spots. It has an eye." Kurt's drawing is an exceptional likeness of the salamander. In the original, colors are subtly blended to show the orange skin, and shading along the "line down its back" gives a three-dimensional appearance. (The reproduction lacks this quality.) Leg configuration, toes, nostrils, and other details are also accurately portrayed. Drawing is an important mode of expression for Kurt and a strength he can share with his classmates. It is also a useful language for recording data.

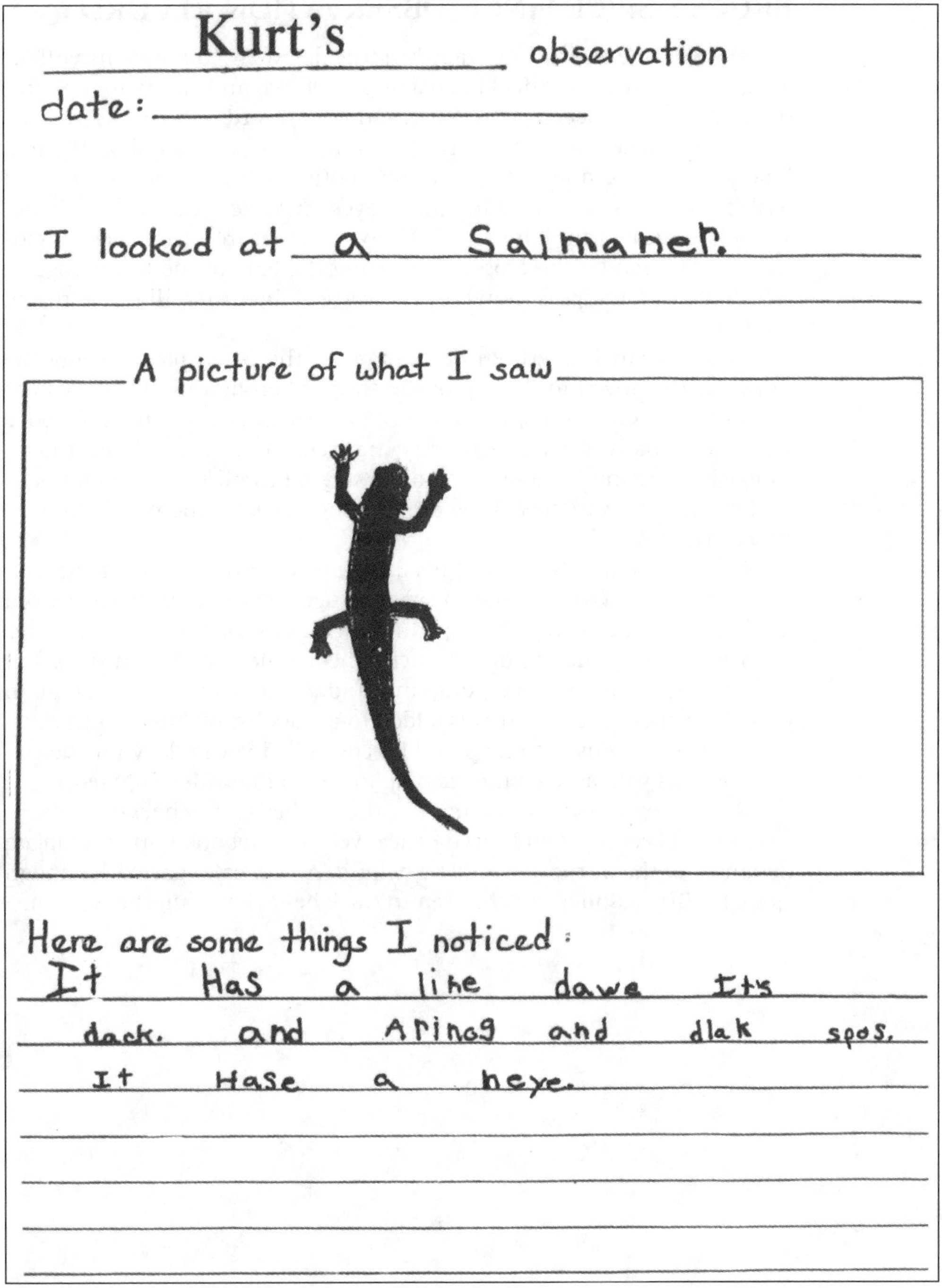

Kurt's _observation

date:_____

I looked at __a_____Salmaner._____

_____

___A picture of what I saw_____

Here are some things I noticed:
It   Has   a   line   dawe   It's
dack.   and   Aring   and   dlak   spos.
It   Hase   a   heye.

Figure 8–9 Kurt's salamander

BRUCE'S SPICE FINCH OBSERVATION RECORD

Bruce (age nine years, one month) struggles with comprehensive language difficulties that affect his reading, spelling, and ability to organize his thoughts in speech or writing. On this record, Bruce has written the word "finches" after "A picture of what I saw" instead of on the line following "I looked at." He has drawn both finches in their purchased basket. Each has a beak, wings, and eyes, and the bird on the left has feathers indicated by faint lines. The woven nature of the nest enclosure is indicated by the crossed lines, and the bars of the larger cage in which the nest hangs is shown by the vertical lines that fill in the rest of the box.

Bruce began his written description in the usual place, below the drawing. He moved to the top of the sheet when he ran out of room at the bottom, then finished his sentence underneath the picture but above what he initially wrote. Here's the transcription: "One of the finch's stomach is getting big and that one is staying in all the time and both of them are in there now. They are making walls for the nest before it's [unclear]."

Bruce has done the bulk of his drawing and writing using a marker. A reminder to use pencil and to leave a finger space between each word might have helped him record his interesting observations more legibly.

The nesting behavior of the finches held Bruce's attention (he spent longer than usual observing, drawing, and writing), and his observation of both finches on the nest was added to a class list of "new" behaviors. Such lists can be used to help build a controlled vocabulary for the science table as well as keep the class up to date on new developments.

Regular opportunities to monitor the finches and a checklist to facilitate record keeping could serve Bruce well. A notebook with a template designed for the purpose would be helpful. A wall calendar with enough space for Bruce and other children to track behavior is another option.

Bruce's _____ observation

date: _____

I looked at _thayo maina wol s for tne he st_ _____

A picture of what I saw _feahes_

Here are some things I noticed _befsets and the Luv the feo hrm a ftumek is eatipo beo and thar lifte irain ol the timy and botnuv tnum lor in tnurhew_

Figure 8–10 Bruce's spice finch

MITCH'S OBSERVATION RECORD OF A STUFFED AND MOUNTED ROBIN

Mitch (age nine years, one month) struggles with oral and written expression. Word retrieval and sustained attention are difficult. Mitch put considerable effort into his drawing of a mount borrowed from a local nature center. He erased several attempts before he was satisfied with the shape he had drawn.

Mitch has shown the long narrow bill, the wing reaching up over the back, and the toes curved around a perch. Colors and markings are basically accurate. He has written, "Its tummy—brick red. It has a little white. They only have black eyes. It has black fingernails. It has grey on its back. It has ugly feet. It eats cherries. 8 1/2 inches." His description focuses first in great detail on the bird's colors. Mitch also includes some information about size and diet that I had read to the class from a book. Specific language and information from the book helps him with his description—"brick red" for the reddish-orange color he notices on the breast, and "cherries" as part of its diet.

Mitch's observation

date: _Sept 24_

I looked at^ r oo d in Mont

___A picture of what I saw___

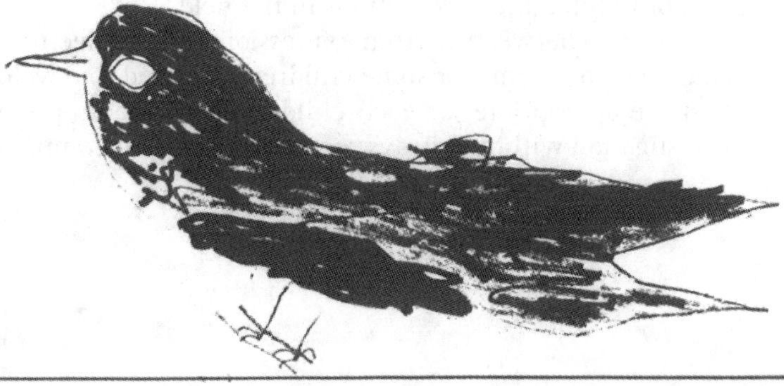

Here are some things I noticed:
1. it's tame brikred it has a
liettile with they on lie have black
eys It has black fagernels It has
grey on it back It has ogle feet
It eys cheares 8 inch's

Figure 8–11 Mitch's robin mount

MARIA'S FEATHER OBSERVATION RECORD

Maria (age nine years, ten months) works to overcome both auditory processing and visual difficulties. Some of her academic skills are more than two years delayed. Expressing herself verbally and sustaining attention are also difficult for her.

Maria has observed a great horned owl feather borrowed from a museum. Both her investment in the project and her artistic ability are evident in her drawing, especially in the way she carefully blended colors to show the feather's markings. She has also written about the pattern: "I noticed it is brown and black on one side and on the top on the other side, brown, yellow, and brown lines. It has black [and] brown lines on it."

Maria's comments during class discussions and fieldwork were often more sophisticated than her written statements on observation records such as this one. Although she struggled to find words to explain her ideas, she was quick to make connections during the course of a discussion or to integrate observations in the field.

The gap between written expression and intellectual understanding can create problems for some children; we need to develop expectations that are appropriate for each child and provide ample opportunity for investigation without always requiring a written component.

Maria's _____ observation

date: Mar. 4 _____

I looked at ___ a fra _____

_____

_____ A picture of what I saw _____

Here are some things I noticed:
I ~~some~~ noticed it is brown
and Black on one side and on
the top on the of side brown
yollon and lan brown, it have Black
brown sns lans on It.

Figure 8–12 Maria's feather

ALLISON'S GUINEA PIG OBSERVATION RECORD

Allison (age eleven) struggles to understand things she hears. She finds conversations, spoken directions, and lectures confusing. Putting her own thoughts into words is far easier. Art is an area of real ability.

Her drawing of the guinea pig is accurate and detailed—pink, folded ears, and fur sticking up along his back and head. She has carefully included the other details of the scene in front of her as well, drawing each plant on the windowsill, the can and the log in the guinea pig's cage, and even water dripping from the water bottle.

Allison has written, "I noticed that it looks like it was blown with a hair dryer for an hour. It has white and brown fur. And little feet that have toenails like needles." This descriptive imagery and the inclusion of the entire scene before her often marked Allison's approach. When science work is not too narrowly defined, there is room for varied interpretations of a task. Children can emphasize different strengths and contribute individual perspectives.

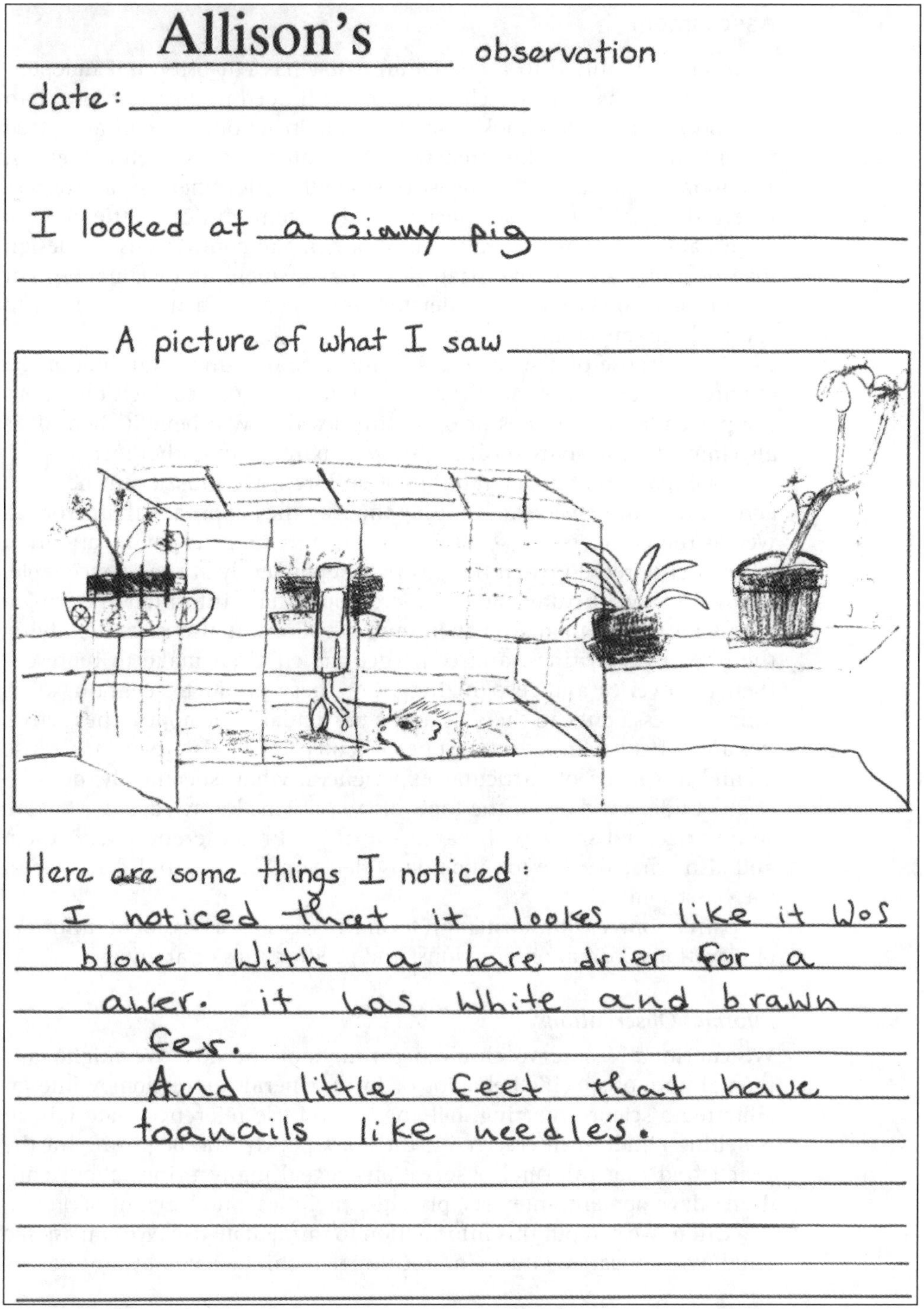

Allison's

observation

date: _____

I looked at __a Ginny pig__

_____ A picture of what I saw _____

Here are some things I noticed:
I noticed that it lookes   like it wos
blone With a hare drier for a
awer. it has White and brawn
fer.
And little feet that have
toanails like needle's.

Figure 8–13   Allison's guinea pig

Assessment

If we are committed to a curriculum that has curiosity and independent thinking as goals for children, we will need to discard more than a preprogrammed textbook approach to instruction; we will also need to discard some time-honored ways of evaluating children's progress. Traditional unit tests may measure student achievement in a program where the goal is to master facts, but they communicate little about a child's ability to observe, raise questions, make connections, or design investigations. Alternative strategies for assessment and evaluation that focus broadly on children's understanding and growth are more likely to reveal these capacities.

The purpose of assessment is to increase our understanding of the children in our classroom so that we can make informed decisions about the particular approaches or opportunities that will benefit them. It is also important to share our insights with parents and other teachers.

To expand our understanding of children, we must examine them across many dimensions, observing the way they approach their work as well as the products they create. In science this means paying attention to what children do when they work independently at the science table, play with sand or water, sit at a microscope, share information during a discussion, or try to answer their own questions. It also means studying the drawings, writings, and constructions children make to represent their discoveries and recognizing what these products "contain." This kind of assessment can show us how a particular child approaches activities and what generates interest or difficulty. It can also reveal the sense a child has made of particular experiences: what, specifically, does he or she understand about the topic of study? This knowledge is what we summarize and share with parents during our conferences with them and also what we use to guide daily decision making and planning in the classroom.

Three sources of information form the basis for assessment: informal observations; formal observations; and product files or archives.

Informal Observations

We continually observe children throughout the day. We might take mental note of specific behavior or form general impressions while facilitating a science meeting, helping a child use reference materials, or watching children interact with the class pet. In the beginning of the year I find that informal observations reveal many things about children's development, interests, priorities, abilities, and learning style.

Often, we can put this information to immediate use. We can assist a child who appears confused or encourage a child excited by a discovery to explore it further. We may also keep notes about these impressions to refer to as the year progresses.

Formal Observations

During formal, or planned, observations we observe and record the activities and comments of individuals or groups of children, focusing on particular aspects of their work or behavior. I generally sit near the children I want to observe, notebook in hand, sometimes interacting with them to probe their thoughts or observe specific behavior, and other times keeping silent so as not to exert much influence on their actions. Each approach yields important but different information.

Formal observations often grow out of informal ones. In our daily work with children, we may be puzzled or intrigued by something and decide to schedule additional time to examine it in more detail. We may also observe at particular intervals, making sure we consider each child in relation to specific goals we have set.

For example, I once focused on "raising questions" as an important goal in a science unit. I wanted children to be able to pose questions of their own, rather than respond only to the questions of others. Since the information I gathered through informal observations did not always allow me to know whether children did so, I decided to look at their questioning skills in a more systematic way.

The need for formal observation also arose with Miles and Cory, the two seven-year-olds in Chapter 2 who spent so much of their time looking at crickets. My impression was that they were conducting research of their own design, but this impression could have been incomplete or inaccurate. To verify that their conversations at the science table were indeed about crickets, and to learn more about their particular interests and ideas, I relied on formal observation.

Product Files or Archives

It is useful to keep a file of each child's products, collected at regular intervals throughout the year. Copies of notebook entries, reports, and drawings, along with photographs or descriptions of models can be included. When we are able to review a collection of products made over time, we often notice patterns or changes in a child's work that might escape us if we looked at products individually, sending each home soon after its completion. A cumulative file also helps us identify progress and accomplishments.

Sometimes we observe things that cause us concern or prompt us to work with a child on a specific issue. Eight-year-old Jeremy handed in an observation of a large bone. "It has bumps," he wrote. "It's neat."

An occasional description of this quality would not have aroused my concern, but my impression was (and the archive verified) that Jeremy's recent work lacked substance. I needed to review my expectations for Jeremy and consider strategies for renewing his investment.

Archives also may reveal something about a child's approach—a particular interest, ability, or style. Peter studied an owl feather, reporting: "On the dark side there are seven stripes. On the light side there are eight stripes." Later, he counted up the number of plates on a box turtle's shell. Another time he recorded the number of teeth in a jawbone. Noticing quantity seemed to be a frequent self-chosen focus—one I could tap during science lessons.

Reviewing a collection of products can deepen our understanding of a particular child and aid us as we plan further work. Children may also maintain files of their own, using them both as references and as records of their growth.

Passing Judgment

I want children to do sophisticated science work of high quality. This includes creating records that are accurate and informative. Yet I caution against "correcting" records. I also avoid applying labels such as *good*, *excellent*, or *poor* that state a general judgment. One reason I take this stand is because the real test of a record's quality is how it functions. I want children to create records they can use to remember and communicate information. I also hope the process of making the record, whether it involves drawing, writing, or listing numbers, will help children focus their attention and think about an object, organism, or situation. In the end, it is not my judgment but the relationship between the student, the subject, and the record that matters most.

Here's an example. Suppose that in the process of drawing a cricket, a boy trying to "fit" the wings onto the body notices that there are not just two but *four* wings on the live insect before him. It is a worthwhile discovery. If, on his final product, I note that the cricket he drew has no antennae or eyes or that his hastily written "wings in two kinds" is not a complete sentence, I've missed the main point. I've also shifted the focus from his discovery to my judgment.

In cases where a child's record contains information I question, it can be productive to discuss our diverging observations or ideas. We can perhaps settle the matter by returning to the object or phenomenon for another look. If I try to settle the matter instead by asserting my authority as teacher, I may encourage children to see science less as a matter of "asking nature" than as a matter of coming up with the "right answers" or guessing what I had in mind.

Striving for Quality

Doing science requires being able to work somewhat independently, interpret findings, and make choices about what to pursue. Ideally, I want each child to develop an internal sense of purpose and be able to compare her effort and products to criteria she has developed herself. However, I am aware that my students may have little experience with the situations I plan to place them in. If there are specific standards or criteria I want them to meet, it is best to be clear about them. If, however, I want children to help forge the standards, then I need to expose them to a range of possibilities and help them articulate the value they find in each. I want to help them strive for excellence, but I don't want to oversimplify the task.

One March, I took a class of five- and six-year-olds for a walk. In a vacant lot behind a grocery store we found a variety of trees and shrubs, still dormant after a New England winter, and collected twigs to bring back to our warm classroom. The plan was to put the twigs in water and see what happened.

The children were very excited about the project. They loved twisting their tongues around the word *botanists*, the term I had introduced to describe us during this phase of our science work, and each happily decorated a label to identify the jar that held his or her very own twigs. Some children even collected extra twigs so that they could "watch one at home."

The children's cheerful attitude continued throughout our first scheduled examination of the twigs, but mine did not. Looking around the room, I saw children approaching their work with chatter and haste—looking quickly, scribbling a sketch, and announcing "I'm done." As they hurried to put the papers on which they had recorded their observations in folders or on the bulletin board, I looked over the drawings. There were budless twigs, branchless twigs, and twigs that looked like porcupines. Through I knew that at this age a certain enthusiastic speediness was to be expected, I also felt that these children were capable of more care and attention than I was seeing and that they would learn more about the twigs if their pace slowed. I had hoped to see them looking more closely, discovering the tiny features and patterns that made each twig unique, and recording what they'd noticed more accurately. After a second, similar session I puzzled over how I could encourage more careful attention without sacrificing the happy enthusiasm.

Before sending children off to observe their twigs a third time, I decided to share two books with them. Both were beautifully illustrated. One had dozens of color plates depicting North American wildflowers; the other contained delicate line drawings of aquatic plants.

ELLEN D.: I brought these special books to show you because I know that you are interested in your botany work. Some botanists, like you, study twigs and trees. Other botanists study different kinds of plants. Can you tell what the botanist who wrote this book was studying?

DENISE: Flowers!

ELLEN D.: Yes. This whole book is about the wildflowers that grow in this country. Just as you are observing and drawing your twigs, the botanist who made this book observed flowers and made pictures to show people how they look.

EDDIE: And they wrote about them.

ELLEN D.: And they wrote about them, too. I'm going to show you a picture from this book. [*I turn to a color plate of violets, flowers I think the children may recognize. Immediately hands go up.*]

CONNIE: Oooh!

PHILLIP: We have those at my house!

AMANDA: They're violets!

JOE: That's a good picture!

LORNA: I have lots of those!

ROY: Yeah—they're violets.

ELLEN D.: You're right! This is a picture of violets. How could you tell?

PHILLIP: 'Cause they're just like the ones at my house.

ELLEN D.: Artists can make all kinds of pictures. But the artist who made this picture of a violet for this wildflower book was trying to show people something particular. This is a science drawing and the artist wanted to show people . . .

SHELLY: How it really looks.

ELLEN D.: Yes. What things about this picture are like a real violet?

PAT: The color. The flowers are purple.

KENNY: Not only purple. In the middle there's a tiny bit of white.

AMANDA: I've seen that!

ELLEN D.: Yes—purple with a tiny bit of white, just like real violets. Anything else?

EDDIE: The leaves!

ELLEN D.: What about the leaves?

EDDIE: They're green.

ANNE: And there's lots of them.

SANDY: They go like this (*makes bending motions*).

We look together at a few more color pictures, the children identifying what makes each painting look like a real flower. We also examine several of the line drawings of aquatic plants. Even without color, these drawings look "real" as well as beautiful. I explain that the books will be available to look at later. I also decide to link them explicitly to the work the children will soon undertake. My hope is that the many things children have noticed and admired about the illustrations may give them new ideas about how to study their own twigs. I don't, however, mean to "set the bar" unattainably high.

ELLEN D.: When you do your botany work today, you can think about the things you will want to show about your twig. What can you use if you want to show the colors?

MICKY: Crayons.

LINDA: Colored pencils.

ELLEN D.: Yes. And what different parts do your twigs have that you could show?

SUZANNE: Buds.

DALE: Little branches.

BRENT: Mine is red.

During the next scheduled science period I sensed a change in the tone of the room. My young botanists remained lively and eager, and there were still a few spills as children hurried to get their jars and paper. Once settled, however, their pace relaxed a bit. I circulated among them, commenting on the detail and realism emerging in their records: "I notice you made lots of branches in your drawing, Connie, just as your twig has lots of branches." "I see you drew the forked shape of your twig, Pat."

A few children called me over to share discoveries. "I noticed that the buds on my two are side-by-side—in pairs," Lorna pointed out. I moved in for a closer look. "Yes. I see that they are! I wonder if all twigs have buds in pairs or just some twigs, like yours?"

I was struck by a dramatic change in the work of a few children. Phillip had been settled and focused for almost fifteen minutes, a striking change from last session's early "I'm done!" His drawing, too, had changed enormously. Before, two purple sticks with no distinguishing features rested in wavy lines of water. This time Phillip had shown two

Figure 8–14a Phillip's twig: first drawing

Figure 8–14b Phillip's twig: third drawing

parallel rows of dark buds, green leaves just unfurling, and reddish-brown bark (see Figure 8–14).

"Phillip!" I exclaimed, "You have shown so much about your twig in this picture!"

"I had to use all these crayons," he explained, indicating a wide array of colors, "because when I looked at my twig, I could see lots of different colors on it."

During our science meeting the next day, Phillip shared his drawing with the class. I held up his twig for comparison. "I noticed that the bark has lots of colors," he read. "I'm ready for questions and comments."

"I like your picture," one classmate stated.

"It's good," nodded another.

"It is a good scientific illustration," I agreed. "What makes a science drawing a good one?"

"If it looks like the real thing," said Eli.

"What can you see on Phillip's real twig that he showed in his drawing?"

"The bud."

"Different colors."

"Those two tiny leaves."

"All those things tell us about Phillip's twig," I agreed.

In our next science session I again felt a change. Children settled quickly to work and commented often to classmates as they noted particular aspects of each twig. As children called me to see their finished records, "I'm done" was largely replaced by other kinds of announcements. "See? I made the buds in pairs, the way they are on my twig." "Guess what? My twig has tiny leaves and they are sticky on the bottom!"

Of course, each child progressed with this work in an individual way. Amanda continued to draw her twigs with an extraordinary number of branches, but she showed the relative sizes of her specimens and sometimes showed the color of the leaves and buds. Dennis still checked the room to reassure himself that he was among the first finished but wrote about a change he had noticed and often lingered to watch another child work. Betsy designed a system for tracking changes, comparing her twig to her previous drawing at the start of each session and noting, then drawing, new developments.

I think of quality work in science as being marked by attention and care. We can provide children at any age with the opportunity to work toward appropriately high standards, rather than establish one specific standard that all children must meet. We can also help children look critically at their own efforts, records, and ways of working. We can invite them to identify the ingredients of "good work" and support them as they try to produce it.

9 *Fieldwork*

A school district once hired me to help implement a new elementary science curriculum featuring prepackaged kits. My assignment was to familiarize teachers with the organisms and activities in a unit on living things. By observing snails or other small animals and constructing terrariums in which they could live, these teachers (and eventually, their students) were to learn about life cycles, habitats, and the needs of living things.

As is often the case, little time was allocated to the preparatory training sessions, so I needed to hit the ground running. The trouble was there was nothing to run with. The science kits had been ordered, but not all of them had arrived. The one on living things was among the missing, and the live animals that were to be observed hadn't been obtained either. The teachers were helping themselves to the complimentary coffee and pastry before I realized the extent of the problem: a classic inservice nightmare. What to do? I wasn't sure. I skipped the beginning of the welcome-and-introduction session in order to buy a little time.

I made a high-speed tour of the grounds surrounding the building with an eye out for possibilities. The usual teachers' parking lot and basketball hoops greeted me: no terrarium furnishings there. To my relief, however, I discovered that the building surrounded a tiny courtyard that was landscaped with a row of evergreen shrubs. Glass doors, locked and alarmed, stood in the way, but a kindly custodian came to my aid. Soon I was in under the shrubbery, more pleased than I can say at the sight of wood lice clambering among the grass blades. There were both sow bugs and pill bugs, at least three different kinds all told. One was midway through a molt, and some were so tiny it took a magnifying glass to really see them. Fabulous! I also found beetles, earthworms, slugs, snails, two types of bees, ants, and some centipedes. I rejoined the group, reassured that we would have live specimens to study.

The teachers were understandably frustrated when they learned about the kit snafu. They were anxious about teaching the new curriculum and wanted to see the materials they would soon be using. They made the best of it, however, and followed me to the courtyard. There, my heart sank for a second time that morning. Not a single bug in sight, not one of any kind. The sun had climbed, drying each drop of dew and baking the ground hard: the courtyard had become an inhospitable place for tiny creatures. But where had they all gone? Surely they must be hiding somewhere. Several teachers and I began to search, turning over stones and large clods of dirt. Nothing. Then we noticed that the surface of one of the larger clods was riddled with tiny holes. Odd. Breaking it open we discovered why: wood lice had sought refuge there.

My reactions to this set of events were complicated. On the one hand, the missing kits testified to an ambitious but undersupported curriculum reform, something these teachers were familiar with and weary of. On the other hand, the courtyard, though small and plain, was a much richer context in which to explore the habits and needs of living things than the terrariums we'd been promised. Animals for us to study were right on hand, no purchase necessary. Furthermore, in the few minutes we had spent outside, we had already discovered evidence of an intriguing adaptation to a sometimes harsh environment. What more could be learned? And what would children learn if given the same chance?

There were so many possibilities! Simply hunting around to find out how many kinds of animals inhabited the courtyard would be a good starting place. Then, the physical structures, habits, and life cycles of different species could be investigated, both through repeated visits to the courtyard and by bringing a few animals indoors. Which species were most common? In what areas of the courtyard were they most numerous? Were there any places that seemed devoid of animal life? Were particular species permanent residents, or did they come and go? At what time of day were they more active? What did they eat? How far down into the soil could animals be found? Was there any microscopic life?

Questions like these would require children to come up with ways to gather and interpret specific information. Sometimes, they would need to identify and control variables. Perhaps they could compare the contents of square-foot plots located in different sections of the courtyard, or lay a transect line across it and see whether habitat changes along its length were associated with the creatures they found at various points. Children might discover interesting animal–plant associations or species they didn't know existed. They would surely build ecological concepts such as "population," "community," "niche," "biodiversity," and "life cycle." The courtyard could fuel their work for months.

Study Your Neighborhood

Many completely humble outdoor settings are well worth investigation. One year I took children on weekly visits to a local pond. The by-product of a construction project, it was little more than a ditch, and a motley assortment of waterfowl were typically afloat there. During our first visit, children learned to recognize individual birds and to identify behaviors as well. Some of this behavior startled and amused the children. For example, the ducks sometimes put their heads down in the water so that only their backs were visible and stayed that way for quite a long time. At other times, they "stood up" and ran across the surface of the water, flapping their wings as they went. There was a lot of stretching and tail wiggling. What did it mean? Did the ducks put their heads down in the water to eat, or for some other reason? Do ducks play, and did they run across the water for fun? Were the geese bossy, as they appeared to be, and were any of the ducks mates or friends? These and many other questions surfaced, not because I raised them, but because children were regularly immersed in a context in which curious things were going on.

I scheduled return trips during lunch and recess to preserve academic blocks, and children became quite efficient in their data collection. They arrived at the pond focused on specific behaviors or particular ducks or geese and knew what information they were looking for. Learning to interpret the birds' activity was a satisfying enterprise, made possible because the pond was so near and accessible.

Cultivate the Science Potential of the School Grounds

I once visited a school in a temperate climate where students had begun a campaign to save tropical rain forests. Someone had designed a beautiful T-shirt and organized a fundraiser: for every three T-shirts sold, an acre of rain forest would be saved. The commitment to preserving a natural resource on another continent was clear and praiseworthy.

Evidence that a similar sensibility guided environmental decisions on the school grounds was hard to find. They were deforested for sure, and the few shade trees and shrubs to be found were mostly exotic species. A small flower garden had been planted in marigolds and petunias, and the large lawn was seeded in grass, clipped short. A lone stalk of milkweed had grown up along a fence, too close to the chain link to be clipped by a mower. Obviously, the priority of the grounds supervisor was not wildlife habitat.

It is incongruous (and fiscally imprudent) to spend money on organisms to raise in the classroom while simultaneously paying for their removal from school property. Likewise, educating children about the ecology of a distant ecosystem while they remain ignorant of the one they walk though every day does them a disservice. There is no better place to study shadows, land use, microclimates, and a host of other worthwhile topics than the average American schoolyard. Typically, however, children and teachers are acquainted with it in a limited way: familiar with its recreational potential but not with its soil, vegetation, or wildlife. And while someone decides how to maintain school grounds, the choices made and the consequences that result are rarely part of the curriculum that children and teachers dwell on.

The work of a second-grade class taught by a colleague stands in contrast. The children became interested in the fate of a piece of town land adjacent to their school property. There was talk of converting this "vacant" lot to a soccer field or skating rink, a prospect that greatly appealed to the children. In either case the existing vegetation would need to be mowed short or perhaps replaced by a hard surface. Their teacher decided the children should learn more about the property in order to understand the potential change, so he had them mark out small, square plots that they could study. They simultaneously marked out plots on the more manicured schoolyard, then tried to gain some sense of what each place was like by investigating these spaces.

One thing children did was to try to establish what grew in each plot. They didn't worry about naming the plants they found, but simply paid attention to appearances and kept track of how many seemingly different kinds there were. They tallied the number of individual plants as well as the apparent species. Of course, small creatures were sometimes found, and the children noted these as well. Occasionally, a plant–animal association emerged.

Over the course of a few weeks, the class used this data to think about the characteristics of the town land and the ways in which development would alter it. They came to regard the site as anything but vacant. It was home to an impressive number of species, especially compared with the schoolyard. Altering it would mean great loss as well as great gain, and the children wrestled with the implications of that possibility. In the end, they decided the lot should be preserved in its present form: there were other places where children could skate and play soccer. They even contacted town officials to share their point of view and the basis for it.

My point is not to say what should be done with a particular piece of town land or school property but to note that the very issues students grapple with when they study distant places are often being played out right around them. Familiarity with the local environment, developed through school science study, can help children make sense of these issues. I also believe that most school grounds have far more potential as outdoor laboratories than they currently achieve. Small changes in grounds-keeping practices would turn a manicured, decorative school-yard into a place where children can conduct investigations and develop science concepts and skills. For example, even a small area left to grow instead of being mowed will become a habitat for insects and other tiny animals. Likewise, more plant life will develop fully and go to seed. Science kits provide related options but in simplified form and at greater cost.

Pursue Playground Mysteries

One winter, Janine noticed something beautiful and mysterious at the edge of the woods where she and her classmates often played at recess. Fallen leaves were frozen in the ice. The spectacular thing was that the leaves were not level with the surface of the ice, but several inches below it. They had, it seemed, melted down into the ice, leaving a leaf-shaped open space above them. After several days of studying these on her own, Janine brought her teacher to see them. He found them as beautiful and intriguing as she did, and summoned the rest of the class. Being a regular visitor at the school that winter, I was summoned as well.

There were many attempts to explain this phenomenon. Some children thought there was heat in the leaf. Because the leaf was hot, it could melt down into the ice. Others disagreed. How could a leaf that was sitting on ice in February have heat in it? It made no sense! And besides, the leaves didn't really feel hot. Their teacher asked if there was anything they could do that might help them learn more about this circumstance. The children decided to try to create their own leaf impressions. If they succeeded, they thought, they'd know how it all worked.

In the days that followed, the children froze pans of ice and put leaves on them, but this did not create impressions like the ones Janine discovered. They tried heating the leaves in a microwave oven and putting them on ice while they were still hot, but this didn't work either. After many such experiments, the children had generated a long list of conditions that do not give rise to leaf impressions, and they were feeling stuck and frustrated.

Their teacher and I realized the children were trying to understand a complicated situation, and that in addition to being inexperienced scientists, they had little understanding of its basic "ingredients." Temperature, time, freezing and melting, absorption and reflection—it was all new territory. Perhaps exploring these phenomena would allow children to develop their ideas or shed some light on the leaf-impression problem. The children were eager to get going and posed many questions they wanted to address (some more connected to the leaf impressions than others). Do all liquids freeze? Even salt water? Does water freeze faster outdoors or in the freezer? Is ice in the shade colder than ice in the sun? And how do you measure cold, anyway? The children continued to theorize about what combination of factors had created the leaf impressions while they designed and carried out simple investigations to learn about making and melting ice. We queried them about their plans and findings. What was different about putting ice in a microwave oven and setting it outside in the sun? Chopped up ice seemed to melt faster than plain, smooth ice—why was what?

As the children carried out indoor investigations, they also continued to look at the various leaf impressions on the edge of the playground. One intriguing observation was that they weren't equally deep. The children wondered about this. Perhaps some of the impressions had just begun to form, while others had been growing over time. This gave one group of children the idea that perhaps they could prevent an impression from developing by putting a coat over a fallen leaf. The coat was soon needed by its owner, but while the experiment lasted, no impression formed. Would one have, eventually? And had the uncovered leaves nearby sunk deeper during the day? It was hard to tell. What would be a good way to measure?

Well into this work, I found a book containing photographs of everyday sights from nature, sights often noticed by children. One showed a stone surrounded by snow, except that the snow had melted in the area immediately surrounding the stone. The text offered an explanation: the dark stone absorbed more solar energy than the more reflective surface of the snow. The stone heated up as a result, in turn warming its immediate surroundings. This information was additional food for thought. Eventually, the children pieced together a story that made sense. When a leaf fell on the ice, it was at first cold. "Then," as one child explained, "the sun comes out. The sun bounces off the ice because it is a light color but the leaf is a lot darker so it soaks up the warmth and melts the ice." Maybe the leaf wouldn't get burning hot, but it might get warm enough to melt a little of the ice it rested on. The resulting water was gone— perhaps it went into the air. Kept up over the course of days—voila! a leaf impression.

Evidence, models, and explanation are three of the fundamental concepts that unify the *Standards*. Mysteries like the leaf impressions demand explanation. Teachers can help children to collect and integrate information from various sources into logical explanations (NRC 1996, 115).

Making Fieldwork Efficient and Effective

Teachers aiming to strengthen the connection between children and the natural world find that nothing has the potential to contribute more powerfully than fieldwork. Removing a soil sample from a plastic bag in a science kit just can't compare with digging one out of the earth.

For many children, however, fieldwork is a rare treat, a shining highlight of their school experiences. It isn't hard to understand why. Planning fieldwork adds to a teacher's already crammed to-do list. There are potential sites to visit, programs to research, people to contact, inflexible aspects of the school schedule to work around, and transportation to arrange. Provisions need to be made for children who become confused, overstimulated, or fatigued. The roles of chaperones, naturalists, docents, or tour guides need to be clarified. And once all these plans are finalized, there is the trip itself. "The kids just go wild!" one teacher lamented. "I have to be on top of them every minute."

In the classroom, children come to rely on predictable routines, boundaries, and assignments. Many of these structures disappear during field trips. In their absence, some children become anxious or act as if class rules have vanished along with the desks, chairs, and daily schedule. A few children may be reluctant to leave their teacher's side; others are all too eager to expand their horizons.

Fieldwork, whether conducted on the far side of the playground or in a museum in another town, challenges both teachers and children. Fortunately, simple measures can ease some of the difficulties, freeing everyone to focus more on the science.

Keep it Local, Short, and Simple

Many schools have limited budgets for buses and the other expenses associated with fieldwork. As a result, teachers plan only a few outings a year, and these become major events. No wonder difficulties arise!

A more productive approach is to make fieldwork a regular thing rather than a special event. I like to take my first trip out of the classroom early in the year and then take the same trip again a short time later. The first time is almost a dress rehearsal—there are always bugs to work out. The second time, children have the drill down and can really get some work done. Repeating outdoor experiences in this manner is possible when trips are local, short, and simple.

One year, the first fieldwork I scheduled was a walk around the block to look for birds. Another year, I took a class to the flower garden at the corner of the schoolyard. In yet another, we didn't even leave the building—we went to the office and the furnace room.

Long ago I came across a study that assessed children's ability to learn in novel settings and in more familiar ones. Specifically, it measured children's learning over a series of visits to a nature center. The results? During a class' first visit, children didn't learn all that much about the things their teachers and the nature center staff wanted them to know. On subsequent visits to the same center, learning increased. After many visits, when the setting had perhaps become too familiar, interest and learning began to wane (Falk and Balling 1980).

The article helped me understand the behavior of school groups visiting the museum where I then worked. It was commonplace to see flocks of children spiraling down the central staircase, spraying into the lobby below like so many pinballs. Students would push a button on an interactive exhibit, then dash off to the next one without waiting to see the results. In the middle of live animal demonstrations, I was regularly interrupted not by a remark about the owl on my shoulder but with, "Where does that door over there go?" or "How big is this place, anyway?"

When placed in a new situation, children devote energy and attention to exploring their surroundings, locating themselves, figuring out what to do and how to act. For some children this is a challenging business; others adjust fairly easily. In either case, while children are busy getting settled, they will have little ability to focus on science. The pattern of waves in the giant "ocean tank" or the difference between white oak trees and red ones aren't top priority. As children grow accustomed to their new surroundings and understand what is expected of them, energy is freed for observation, investigation, and instruction.

In essence, a field trip is not really very different from the first day of school. On that first day, children enter the classroom excited, nervous, wary, or unsure. We could greet them with a lecture about the parts of a flower or send them off to do a chemistry experiment—but most of us don't. Instead, we offer time to explore the room, learn the names of classmates, find the coatroom and the bathroom. Fieldwork requires an adjustment to a new setting, too. Below are some techniques and ways of thinking that can make fieldwork more effective and efficient.

Anticipate What Students Need to Know

I introduce classroom activities with deliberation and care, making sure children are aware of my specific expectations. Fieldwork can be introduced in the same way. I sometimes meet with children and solicit ideas about what fieldwork is, then proceed from general definitions to focusing on specific assignments or behavior that will enable us to do some science.

Practice Safety Procedures Ahead of Time

If we are to take children out of the classroom responsibly, we need to feel confident that we can keep the class together and safe. Having plenty of adult chaperones along is part of planning for safety and so is knowledge of the particular place we are going. It helps to know whether there is cell phone coverage, drinkable water, or poison ivy. It also helps to know that we can count on the children to follow directions, stay with the group, come when we call, and help one another.

Before any trip away from the classroom, even one to a location just outside the building, teach any special signals or procedures you'll be using. I find the same ones I use indoors and on the playground are sufficient for most trips. Raising my hand means "freeze and listen." If I say "circle up," everyone comes to where I am standing and forms a circle. Sometimes each child has a number, or a partner, so that we can count off and quickly learn if anyone is missing. When I see that children can do these things easily and quickly indoors, I'm ready to try fieldwork on the playground. If that goes smoothly, I feel confident that we can go farther.

Some outdoor activities demand a great deal of responsibility from children. Boat trips, difficult hikes, and overnight campouts are examples. I prepare children for these, but if the trip date is fast approaching and I don't feel confident that safety procedures have been internalized, I postpone or restructure the trip.

Outdoor investigations require children to do many things at once: focus, observe, listen, question, keep track of materials, keep track of the rest of the class, cooperate with a group, and adjust to unanticipated changes in plans. These varied jobs can be taken on separately and practiced ahead of time.

Emphasize the Familiar

If children are comfortable observing objects or discussing ideas in the classroom, they can move on to new settings such as the playground, the park, or the woods and continue to do that work well. By varying just one major condition at a time, we allow children to draw on their experience and competence as they tackle something new. If we change the setting, the nature of the assignment, and the rules and expectations all at once, the job becomes much more difficult. Few children will be able to do what we ask of them in such instances. The more novel (or difficult) the new setting is, the more comfortable the work needs to be. The presence of familiar structures (such as oft-used recording forms) may be reassuring for some children and help them focus.

A teacher I knew worked at a nature center where school groups attended weeklong sessions. A night hike was usually one of the activities.

Figure 9–1   Students recording observations in notebooks

Children, guided by one of the center's staff, walked in the woods to listen for animal sounds, stargaze, and learn the patterns of some of the easier-to-locate constellations. But before heading for the woods, this teacher sat with the children near the camp buildings, passed out paper and crayons, and let them color. It wasn't very "sciency," perhaps not even very sensible (coloring in the dark?), but, as she explained, "It's a big deal, being out in the dark. It's scary, and these kids are only ten or eleven; they're away from home; they're not used to the woods; and I'm not even their regular teacher! So we color. Everybody knows how to color!" Simple, concrete things that can help maintain a sense of stability and predictability are keeping class rules in force; following lunch, recess, or meeting routines; and using familiar recording forms or work materials. (See Figure 9–1.)

Establish Boundaries

Within the classroom, familiar boundaries tell children what to do. The walls define a space within which certain things are expected. When we leave the classroom, we need to establish new boundaries. This is particularly important in places that can feel enormous or frightening to a child (a deep woods, the night, or an unfamiliar part of the city). Sometimes

Figure 9–2   **Student observing in plot outdoors**

we can physically mark or walk off boundaries. Children may like to explore a plot of ground after they've marked its perimeter with string (see Figure 9–2), or it might help to hear, "You can do your observation anywhere in this field—but you need to stop at the tree line."

Sometimes the boundaries have less to do with a particular space and more to do with staying together. On trips, I expect us to remain together as a group. For each trip, we define and practice how we will do that, whether that means always keeping me in sight, exploring within whistle range, or walking next to a partner on the sidewalk.

Set Clear Expectations

Children in the classroom need to know what is expected of them. They need to know the teacher's responsibilities and their responsibilities, where there is choice and where there is not. Out of the classroom, this kind of clarity is equally important, but it may be more difficult to achieve. Collaborating with the other adults involved to establish the general purpose, specific work, and any rules for each trip is important.

We can work with parent chaperones, tour guides, and instructors to make rules and roles clear. Chaperones may need advance permission to take charge in situations when teachers are not available (for instance, when the noise level in the car becomes too loud for safe driving). While we can share our instructional role with a guide, we nevertheless remain in charge of our classes, responsible for tone, discipline, and safety.

Clear consequences may need to accompany clear expectations. In the classroom, we can discuss our expectations for how children will work together and what steps we will take when children forget or test rules the class has established. Before we move work out of the classroom, we need to think through not only our expectations but what assistance we are prepared to give children who struggle with those expectations and what consequences will result if the expectations aren't met.

Fieldwork that is part of ongoing study has more meaning than trips seen as isolated occurrences. In preparing for such work, teacher and children need to discuss the connection between what happens in the field and what happens in the classroom: one fuels the other. We may follow a bird-watching trip with an afternoon of watercolor painting or journal writing; collect pond creatures for further study in the classroom; or construct a model or write a report, song, or story using data gathered outdoors.

A Framework for Successful Field Trips

- Start small—with short, simple, local trips.

- Turn routine outdoor moments into fieldwork opportunities. (For example, lining up after recess provides a moment to check cloud cover or watch birds.)

- Practice safety procedures and unfamiliar aspects of the fieldwork.

- Become familiar with the site and anticipate possible difficulties. (Check on laws and regulations that may restrict certain outdoor activities such as collecting.)

- Keep in mind the difference between working in novel and familiar settings.

- Establish boundaries in the new setting and maintain as much stability as possible.

- Establish clear expectations for children's work and behavior, as well as clear roles for adults.

- Establish consequences for inappropriate behavior.

- Follow up fieldwork and integrate it with classroom work, strengthening children's connection to their surroundings and developing their curiosity.

- Don't forget, fieldwork isn't mainly about rules and trouble-shooting. It's about giving children the chance to learn about the world. Well-managed trips make that possible.

A Final Word

If we intend to inspire children to inquire and investigate, we must first make sure we are doing those things, too. If our early science experiences have resulted in a sense of ourselves as people who can figure things out, we are fortunate. We are poised to share our curiosity and confidence with children. But if our early experiences leave us feeling that science is confusing, boring, or beyond us, we may have to work to discover the interest and ability we think we lack. Whatever our backgrounds, we need to observe, wonder, ponder, take note of patterns, and search for connections. Like the students we teach, we will learn as a result of our own activity—our own struggle to make sense of what we see.

I believe that teachers should get to explore in the kind of climate I have talked about creating for children. We need the freedom to question and experiment, and we need others who will attend to our efforts and help us as we search for new understanding. Providing these things for ourselves often proves a great deal more difficult than doing so for students, but it is an important step to take for their sakes as well as for our own. Strengthening our own connection to the world around us is the first step in strengthening theirs.

Name: _____ Date: _____

I looked at _____

┌───┐
│   │
│   │
│   │
│   │
│   │
│   │
│   │
│   │
│   │
│   │
└───┘

I noticed _____

_____

Name: _____ Date: _____

I looked at _____

I noticed _____

_____

I wonder _____

Name of scientist _____

I looked at _____

I noticed _____

_____

_____

_____

_____

_____

Name: _____ Date: _____

I looked at _____

_____

_____ A picture of what I saw _____

Here are some things I noticed:

_____

_____

_____

_____

_____

Name: _____

Date: _____

What happens _____

References

Abell, Sandra, and Mark Volkman. 2006. *Seamless Assessment in Science*. Portsmouth, NH: Heinemann.

Ackerman, Edith. 1990. "From Decontextualized to Situated Knowledge: Revisiting Piaget's Water-Level Experiment." *Epistemology and Learning Group Memo No. 5*. Massachusetts Institute of Technology Media Lab.

Atwell, Nancy, ed. 1990. *Coming to Know*. Portsmouth, NH: Heinemann.

Calkins, Lucy. 1986. *The Art of Teaching Writing*. Portsmouth, NH: Heinemann.

Campbell, Brian, and Lori Fulton. 2003. *Science Notebooks*. Portsmouth, NH: Heinemann.

Clayton, Marlynn, with Mary Beth Forton. 2001. *Classroom Spaces That Work*. Turners Falls, MA: Northeast Foundation for Children.

Cohen, Elaine Pear, and Ruth Straus Gainer. 1995. *Art: Another Language for Learning*, Third Edition. Portsmouth, NH: Heinemann.

Duckworth, Eleanor. 1978. *The African Primary Science Program*. Grand Forks, ND: North Dakota Study Group on Evaluation.

———. 1996. *The Having of Wonderful Ideas*, Second Edition. New York: Teachers College Press.

Edwards, Carolyn, Lella Gandini, and George Forman, eds. 1993. *The Hundred Languages of Children*. Norwood, NJ: Ablex Publishing Corporation.

Eisner, Elliot. 1983. "On the Relationship of Conception to Representation." *Art Education* (March): 22–27.

Erikson, Erik. 1950, 1963. *Childhood and Society*, Second Edition. New York: W. W. Norton and Company.

Falk, John, and John D. Balling. 1980. "The School Field Trip: Where You Go Makes the Difference." *Science and Children* (March): 6–8.

Furman, Rich. 2007. *Practical Tips for Publishing Scholarly Articles*. Chicago: Lyceum Books.

Gallas, Karen. 1994. *The Languages of Learning*. New York: Teachers College Press.

———. 1995. *Talking Their Way into Science*. New York: Teachers College Press.

Harlen, Wynne. 2001. *Primary Science: Taking the Plunge*, Second Edition. Portsmouth, NH: Heinemann.

Hawkins, David. 2002. *The Informed Vision*. New York: Algora Publishing.

Hein, George, and Sabra Price. 1994. *Active Assessment for Active Science*. Portsmouth, NH: Heinemann.

Jackman, Wilbur. 1904. *Third Yearbook of the National Society for the Scientific Study of Education, Part 2, Nature-Study*. Chicago: University of Chicago Press.

McGlashan, Patricia, et al. 2007. *Outdoor Inquiries*. Porstmouth, NH: Heinemann.

Mitchell, Lucy Sprague. 1971. *Young Geographers*. New York: Bank Street College of Education.

National Research Council. 1996. *National Science Education Standards*. Washington, DC: National Academy Press.

Oxford Scientific Films. 1979. *The Chicken and the Egg*. New York: Putnam.

Piaget, Jean. 1980. *To Understand Is to Invent*. New York: Penguin Books.

Pratt, Carolyn. 1948. *I Learn from Children*. New York: Simon and Schuster. New edition: New York: Harper and Row, 1990.

Project Zero and Reggio Children. 2001. *Making Learning Visible*. Reggio Emilia, Italy: Reggio Children.

Seefeldt, Carol. 2005. *How to Work with Standards in the Early Childhood Classroom*. New York: Teachers College Press.

Shamos, Morris. 1995. *The Myth of Scientific Literacy*. New Brunswick, NJ: Rutgers University Press.

Smith, Nancy, and the Drawing Study Group. 1998. *Observation Drawing with Children*. New York: Teachers College Press.

Sobel, David. 1996. *Beyond Ecophobia*. Great Barrington, MA: The Orion Society.

Strachota, Bob. 1996. *On Their Side*. Greenfield, MA: Northeast Foundation for Children.

Wadsworth, Barry. 1978. *Piaget for the Classroom Teacher*. New York: Longman.

Wood, Chip. 1994. *Yardsticks*. Greenfield, MA: Northeast Foundation for Children.